AGE

NOTES

including
- *Introduction to the Novel*
- *Recurrent Themes in the Novel*
- *Style*
- *Character Analyses*
- *Critical Commentaries*
- *Questions for Review*

by
Frank B. Huggins

INCORPORATED

LINCOLN, NEBRASKA 68501

Editor

Gary Carey, M.A.
University of Colorado

Consulting Editor

James L. Roberts, Ph.D.
Department of English
University of Nebraska

ISBN 0-8220-0930-7
© Copyright 1963
by
C. K. Hillegass
All Rights Reserved
Printed in U.S.A.

1993 Printing

The Cliffs Notes logo, the names "Cliffs" and "Cliffs Notes," and the black and yellow diagonal-stripe cover design are all registered trademarks belonging to Cliffs Notes, Inc., and may not be used in whole or in part without written permission.

Cliffs Notes, Inc.   Lincoln, Nebraska

CONTENTS

INTRODUCTION

IN SUMMARY *Of Human Bondage* sounds like a story that hardly moves at all. In the sense that a Dumas book or a paperback adventure novel moves, this is true. There is no physical action, and the plot is simply the story of one man's struggle to find himself in a cruel world.

Philip, the protagonist, who we presume is Maugham himself, is an orphan with a club-foot. But he is not badly off financially, and he has a keen mind.

Maugham, so far as is known, has never completely admitted that this book is autobiographical. He says this in the introduction to one of its many editions:

At the time *Of Human Bondage* was written many novelists, possibly incited by the deep impression made on them by Samuel Butler's *The Way of All Flesh,* were impelled to write semi-autobiographical novels. I say semi-autobiographical because of course they were works of fiction and it was the right of the authors to alter the facts they were dealing with as they chose. Such a book was *Of Human Bondage.* When I made up my mind to write it I was a popular playwright and much in demand; I retired from the theater for a couple of years because I knew that by writing it I could rid myself of a great number of unhappy recollections that had not ceased to harrow me. This it did.

From what is known of Maugham's life, it appears that the early portions of the book are purely autobiographical, with certain changes of scene. Maugham did not have a club-foot, but he was an orphan. He spent his early years in Paris, and his English was stilted, in addition to which he stammered. Sometime during his medical education, Maugham apparently had an unhappy love affair. It must have been with some girl who resembled Mildred. Mildred is almost frighteningly too real to be a product of any writer's imagination; she must have been drawn from real life.

Maugham admits that there may be passages and episodes in *Of Human Bondage* that are too personal to be of general interest. Depending on how one reacts, this may be true. It is certainly a very long story, and some critics have said that the book could have been half the length. There is a novel within a novel, and when it was adapted for the screen some years ago with Leslie Howard and Bette Davis taking the main parts, the scenario writer discarded the wrapping and kept the core. It was an outstanding motion picture.

This is without doubt the most subjective of Maugham's novels or short stories. The Old Observer is here involved in the story himself, and while occasionally he manages to look at the passing scene from outside, in this book he is generally inside looking out. However, it should be noted that in building Philip step by step into an observer, Maugham seems to be showing us how he became the reporter he is. For in his later writings, we get the impression that he never injects himself into the story, except possibly in philosophical asides.

It has been said that one of the dangers of becoming acquainted with Maugham is that you will find yourself depicted in one of his stories. How true this is, only those involved can say, but certainly in this one book, Maugham himself is the central character, Philip Carey.

SUMMARY OF THE PLOT

Philip Carey, the protagonist, is a club-foot orphan. The story is laid in England, Germany, and France in the years between 1885 and around 1905.

The death of his mother, as the story opens, leaves Philip an orphan at the age of nine, and he goes to live with his aunt and uncle, the Vicar of Blackstable. He is then sent to King's School, presumably to study for the clergy. As a cripple he does not have an easy life at school nor in his dealings with people in general. He is a lonely, introverted boy, sensitive and intelligent.

Philip has a little money he inherited from his mother, but it is barely enough to see him through until he masters a profession, which, as a gentleman in England at the time, is the only course left to him.

Philip hates the life at school and when he is 18 he leaves to spend a year in Germany. After he returns to England, he tries to become an accountant but finds he has no head for it. Because he has some talent with drawing, he decides to go to Paris and study art. After two years he discovers his talents are limited.

On returning to England again, he takes up the study of medicine, his father's profession.

He meets Mildred who at the time is a waitress. She becomes the obsession of his life, and the major part of the book is devoted to his relations with her. Mildred is coarse and indifferent to Phillip and not particularly attractive, but Philip falls madly in love with her. The love is not returned, but Philip will do anything for her.

Mildred has a child by another man and she has an affair with one of

Philip's friends, but all through this he is not able to rid her from his heart. This is the bondage of the title, the slave to passion that Philip is. He looks after her even when he discovers she has become a prostitute, but when Mildred turns the tables and tries to seduce him, he spurns her, and she leaves. He feels free at last, but he sees her once more; by now she is dying of a venereal disease.

Philip's fortunes drop and he loses all his money. For a time he works as a shopwalker, but after the death of his uncle he inherits enough to continue his medical education. After graduation he has plans to go abroad, but instead he falls in love with the daughter of his dearest friend, and as the book ends Philip is about to be married.

RECURRENT THEMES IN THE NOVEL

This is one of the great books written about a man's bondage to love, or passion. It depicts in a clear and unrelenting manner the thralldom of one man to a worthless woman. There are sub-plots, but essentially it is the story of unrequited love, of passion on the part of one that is not returned in kind.

It is, at times, an almost embarrassing book. There are passages and scenes that no thoughtful reader can pass over without mentally writhing. How can a man sink so low in his passion, he may ask? And yet, at the same time, he will probably have an uncomfortable feeling that the same thing could happen to anyone, including himself. A look at newspaper headlines will show that it is happening every day. Only the setting has been changed.

Maugham spares no one, including himself. This is a brutally frank story, and a very moving one. It is not a novel to be casually read and tossed aside. Maugham, the great storyteller, constantly disclaims any intention of writing a novel for anything but entertainment; but in this—probably his greatest work—there is a deep message that the reader can hardly ignore.

The word is ambivalence. The dictionary tells us that this is: "Simultaneous attraction toward and repulsion from an object, person, or action." This is the recurring theme throughout the book: love and hate, good and bad, happiness and sorrow, prosperity and poverty. There is hardly a chapter where some aspect of this contrast is not brought out.

In essence, what Maugham is telling us here, and in all his works, for that matter, is that no man is all good nor all bad, that there is no such thing as all-love and all-hate in human relationships. That is why we are humans. As Philip, the protagonist, says at one point:

"What a price it was to pay for being other than the beasts!"

STYLE

Maugham's writing style is essentially a simple one. He does not embellish with sonorous phrases, nor does he lean on the adjective. He is a reporter, and a very good one. He tells a story; he draws no morals, and he leaves it at that. Maugham has said that he is a teller of tales, a professional writer, and that it is his job to entertain the reader. This is exactly what he does, and he has done it so well for over half a century that he is one of the most successful writers in the world.

His style, or perhaps one might say his lack of style, is one of the reasons why, despite his enormous and generally superior output over the years, he has never been recognized as a truly great writer in the sense that a Hemingway or a Joyce or a Gide is accepted. Maugham, the master reporter, will spin for you an entertaining tale, and in many cases it is far more than a simple story. He leaves it to you, however, to read into it whatever you wish. Let the psychologists and the sociologists and others argue about what lies behind the story. All Maugham does is to chronicle what are, in most instances, plain facts. Names and places have been changed and a tight-knit story has been built up from what was possibly an incident he was told about, but only rarely—and perhaps never—does Maugham concoct a plot from whole cloth. He is a chronicler, and his style is that of a crack reporter.

Of Human Bondage is plainly autobiographical in nature, but it is not a rambling, disjointed story, as most autobiographies are apt to be. The novel is a masterfully planned, professional piece of work, and plainly that of a writer who has been disciplined by writing for the stage.

While this may be over-simplification, it is said in playwriting that ideally a character should be introduced beforehand, then again be brought to the attention of the audience before his ultimate entrance. (Shakespeare is a master at this technique.) A basic and rather horrible example might go like this:

MARY: When did you say that Ralph, the playboy millionaire, was coming?

JOHN: He should be here shortly. He's driving up from Tuxedo Park in his Jaguar XK140-E.

MARY: Oh, really. (Pause) What's that I hear? Thunder at this time of year?

JOHN: (Cocking an ear) No, that's quadruple pots. It's a Jag.

(Offstage squealing of brakes, then the door bursts open and RALPH enters.)

And so forth.

Maugham is hardly so obvious, but he is a master at setting the scene. Each portion of the novel fits into the next, and nothing is accidental or haphazard. It has all been carefully and skillfully plotted.

Anyone interested in Maugham's style would do well to read the first few chapters of *The Summing Up,* a factual book in which he talks of many things. Of his own writing style he has a great deal to say, but it is perhaps summarized best in a short statement he makes:

> I knew that I should never write as well as I could wish, but I thought with pains I could arrive at writing as well as my natural defects allowed. On taking thought it seemed to me that I must aim at lucidity, simplicity and euphony. I have put these three qualities in the order of importance I assigned to them.

Maugham has a great deal more to say about style, but the above are the three qualities he has in all his writings. They are qualities that any city editor would welcome in his reporters. Maugham is a great reporter. What also makes him a great fictioneer is his ability to see drama in everyday life. And finally, Maugham is the old pro, the true writer, who year after year can turn out everything from plays to novels to essays. Writing is his profession and he has mastered it. He is like the pinch hitter who can come off the bench and deliver in the clutch, or the basketball veteran who can dunk that free throw when it is needed the most.

No young writer can go far wrong in studying Maugham's pure style. It does not ring with the magnificent music of Thomas Wolfe, nor does it have the distinctiveness of Ernest Hemingway, but it is clean and direct and honest — lucid, simple, and euphonic.

CHARACTERS

(There are perhaps 100 characters who appear in this long novel. The ones listed below are those who have any direct or even indirect bearing on the main plot itself.)

Philip Carey
The protagonist. The novel is the story of his life from the age of nine to about 30.

William Carey
Philip's uncle, the Vicar of Blackstable, selfish, hard, but not consciously cruel.

Mrs. Carey
The Vicar's wife, a kind, gentle, and loving woman.

Mr. Perkins
  Headmaster of King's School, a brilliant scholar, not a "gentleman."

Rose
  Schoolfriend of Philip, an extroverted, popular, athletic type.

Hayward
  Amateur art critic, dilettante friend of Philip, first encountered in Heidelberg.

Emily Wilkinson
  Spinster governess with whom Philip has his first affair.

Fanny Price
  Completely untalented, incompetent art student in Paris.

Clutton
  Talented art student in Paris.

Lawson
  Competent artist, first encountered in Paris. One of Philip's closest acquaintances.

Cronshaw
  Bohemian British poet type, an amateur philosopher and conversationalist.

Mildred Rogers
  The female protagonist, common, arrogant, unattractive London slut.

Miller
  German immigrant in London, a typical, crass traveling salesman type who has an affair with Mildred.

Norah Nesbit
  Charming young woman who writes pot-boilers for a precarious living. Loves Philip.

Macalister
  Stockbroker who plays an important part in Philip's financial life.

Griffiths
  Medical student friend of Philip who has an affair with Mildred.

Athelny
  Bombastic little journalist who ultimately becomes Philip's dearest friend.

Mrs. Athelny
Athelny's wife, a kindly, simple, unassuming woman, the mother of nine.

Sally
Oldest of Athelny's brood — sweet, honest, strong, and affectionate.

Dr. South
Country doctor who takes a liking to Philip.

CHAPTER SUMMARIES AND COMMENTS

CHAPTERS I THROUGH IV

SUMMARY

The novel opens in London in 1885 with Philip Carey, a small boy with a club-foot, being summoned to see his mother, who is dying after having given birth to a still-born child. After a brief time with her in bed, he is taken to stay with his godmother, Miss Watkins. A week later, after the death of his mother, he is brought home again by his nurse, Emma, to meet his uncle, the Vicar William Carey, older brother of Philip's father, who had died six months previously. Philip is to go and live with him in Blackstable, some 60 miles from London. The Vicar has been married for 30 years but is childless. Both he and his wife are kindly people, but they do not look forward to having a small boy underfoot. Although Philip's father was a surgeon in good standing, he left very little when he died, and Philip has about 2,000 pounds to last him until he can earn his own living. He journeys with his uncle to the vicarage in Blackstable.

COMMENT

In these short opening chapters Maugham sets the scene for the bleak world in which a crippled child of nine finds himself after the death within six months of both his father and mother. From the very first page the reader feels a sense of tragedy. The mother is obviously very ill and is being granted a last wish to see her son. Also, by the act of stroking her son's foot in bed, we learn that he has a club-foot. There is a general sense of hopelessness about the opening, and this is heightened by the doctor in attendance, who, behind a screen in the sickroom, takes a look at the still-born baby who is the cause of Mrs. Carey's condition. As the chapter ends, the final note of tragedy is sounded as the still-sleeping Philip is taken away to stay with his godmother, and the nurse asks the doctor if there is any hope. The answer is negative.

There is never any overt cruelty against the little boy in these opening passages, but the loneliness of his situation is made crystal clear. When he returns from his godmother's with his nurse, Emma, to meet his uncle, the Vicar, with whom he is to stay, he is told that Emma cannot go with him. We are led to understand that this is the final break with his past. He is permitted to take all his toys, and also one thing that belonged to his parents. Philip picks a clock he knew his mother liked, then goes to her room for a last look. He pulls open the drawers of a cabinet and looks at his mother's things, and he throws his arms around her dresses, and lies on her bed.

Except when he is parted from Emma, Maugham never indicates that the newly orphaned boy cried of his own volition, and by underplaying the melodramatic, by showing a well-behaved little Victorian boy reacting in a still-upper-lip manner of the time, conveys more of a deep sense of tragedy than would have been the case otherwise. But the bleak world that lies ahead for Philip is established. We know that he had had luxuries that he will no longer have; we know that he has lost a mother that he loved and who loved him.

The opening chapters are particularly important for a full understanding of the events to come. Maugham is skillfully laying the seeds for the crop that will follow.

Philip Carey is not an orphan in the slums of London. He is not starving, nor is he beaten. He is not an Oliver Twist. But we are led to understand that he is a young gentleman in somewhat straitened circumstances and will have to live in a different manner in the future.

By the time Chapter IV ends we find that Philip has gone through his first day at the vicarage. Maugham has succeeded in establishing that the little boy is entering into a very lonely life among adults who, while they do not dislike him, neither want him nor really love him — even though they may wish to. The stage for what is to follow has been masterfully set.

NOTES

Godmother
A female sponsor at the time of baptism in the Church of England (Episcopal Church in the United States) who guaranteed his or her religious education. This was generally an older friend of the family. There was also a godfather.

Red Indian
This is the British for what we call an [American] Indian. What we call a Hindu is what the British call an Indian.

Two Thousand Pounds

The subject of money will occur time and time again throughout the book and it will be useful to have some idea of the sums referred to in reference to present day values and their buying power. The pound—the top British gold unit of money—of the period was equivalent to five United States gold dollars. This was a time when laborers in this country received about a dollar for a 12-hour day. Philip's 2,000 pounds was therefore worth $10,000 in gold. Invested wisely, it was theoretically enough to keep him reasonably comfortable for the rest of his days. It was by no means a large fortune, but at least something that should keep him from starving.

Nursery Tea

Tea is another word that will occur frequently. It has no reference to the beverage, although it was—and is—generally drunk "at tea." Tea is a meal of sorts and one that does not exist in this country in the sense that Maugham refers to it. In order to understand its significance, one must know that in Victorian days the big meal of the day was taken around midday. Then, at some time around five or six in the afternoon, tea was served—or eaten. Depending on the class of the people involved—and again it should be remembered that this novel is not set in a classless society, but one that still held rigidly to class lines—tea was or was not the final meal of the day. For the laboring man, it definitely was; it was bread and butter and cheese and possibly a bit of meat and a glass of beer that he had on returning from work. For the upper classes—the nobility and the rich—it could be a three o'clock snack of small sandwiches and cakes to be followed at around eight by another meal, to be called either dinner or supper—the former if the midday meal was not the main one of the day. In the upper middle-class society in which Philip was reared, tea was quite likely a substantial meal, and for the young, the last meal of the day before retiring. Adults might or might not have a light supper later. In general it might be said that tea took on more importance the lower you were in the social scale. The term "high tea" always referred to a tea at which meat was served, and was quite definitely a substantial, if simple, meal.

Antimacassar

Dandies of the day daubed their hair with that "greasy kid stuff" that was known as Macassar oil, and ladies draped the backs of chairs and couches with lacy cloth that could be removed and washed. They can still be seen in places.

Top of the Egg

Here again tea is something more substantial than just tea and cakes. In this case the Vicar alone is having a soft-boiled egg, but after he has knocked the top off his egg with his spoon he offers the top—with a slight amount of the white left in it—to Philip. This was common practice in Britain, and while hardly satisfying to the youthful recipient, made him feel he was sharing in an adult treat.

2

CHAPTERS V THROUGH IX

SUMMARY

These chapters tell of life in the vicarage in Blackstable. Philip discovers that he is no more lonesome than he was formerly. He is used to being an only child, and he settles into the routine of the vicarage without rebelling against any of them. The story takes him through the summer and we learn that Philip is quite a reader and that his "brain was precocious." His uncle and aunt, seeing that he is able to busy himself, pay little attention to him. But on a Sunday when he is ordered by his uncle to learn a short prayer, selected for the day, and is unable to do so, he breaks out crying and his aunt hears him. Her heart is touched, for she had never imagined before that he was lonely and unhappy. Through her he is introduced to more books in the Vicar's library—books which the Vicar himself does not read. He gets to read, among other things, a good many novels that he enjoys. He develops the habit of reading.

COMMENT

The plot is not advanced in these chapters, but Maugham draws a penetrating picture of a country vicarage in Victorian England. What we see is a colorless routine of honest, God-fearing folk, content in the main, to be what they are. There is a brief flashback in which Mrs. Carey, Philip's mother, appears to be an emotional woman who wishes to leave her son some last photographs although she knows she is dying. The contrast between this romantic gesture and the drab life of the vicarage based on pragmatic virtues is clearly evident. The author also shows us how tyrannical, if not self-imposed, the life of a Victorian gentleman of the times was. The Vicar, while not castigated, is depicted as a self-centered, selfish martinet. On the other hand, his wife, Philip's aunt by marriage, is shown to be a typical wife of the times, bowing to her husband in all matters—or seeming to do so—but a woman with a warm heart who would like to have borne children. While she is unable to give Philip the affection she would like because of her reticence, she is fond of the boy—and this becomes clear in later chapters. Philip, on his part, finds affection in Mary Ann, the maid-of-all-work. As the chapters end, the Vicar is thinking of sending Philip off to school.

In Chapter IX, we see Philip break down completely for the first time. Actually, the misery is simply a compounding of all that has gone before, and the incident itself is relatively unimportant. It does bring out, however, that his aunt loves him in her own way, although she is unable to convey it to a small boy as she might wish. Maugham also brings out that while the uncle is not a cruel man he has absolutely no idea of how to deal with his nephew. "What's he got to cry about?" he asks, and this, in a sense, summarizes his feelings. "He felt extraordinarily helpless," we are told.

After Philip learns to find solace in books, Maugham introduces a philosophy that he mentions many times in his other writings. The habit of reading, according to Maugham, is like an addiction to drugs. He says that it is the most delightful of all habits, but at the same time one that takes a person into an unreal world and makes the real world of every day a source of bitter disappointment.

In his later years, in *The Summing Up, Teller of Tales,* and other autobiographical writings, Maugham will refer again and again to this reading phobia.

NOTES

Shilling
There are 20 shillings to the pound. At this time the shilling was worth 25 cents.

The Times
This is *The Times* of London, the venerable "Thunderer" that some still consider the greatest newspaper in the world. It is not to be confused with other *Times,* where the definitive article is not used. There is only one *The Times.*

Chapel
The reference here is to Protestant sects other than the Church of England. The "church" is the Church of England church.

Bath
The story is laid in a period almost a century ago, and sanitary habits were not what they are today. Plumbing was also primitive. In Britain it still is.

Fly
A light carriage for hire. Somewhat like a taxi today.

Penny or Pence
There are 12 pennies to a shilling—and you may recall there are 20 shillings to a pound. So at this period a pence was worth about two cents.

Florin
A silver coin worth two shillings.

Harbour
This is not a typographical error. The British still spell harbour, labour, arbour, humour and so forth with the added "U." But our advertising writers also write "glamour" instead of "glamor" so perhaps it is more glamourous.

Licking Into Shape
Not quite the American meaning of beating into shape, but an indication that discipline is needed.

Popish
Anything that smacked of Roman Catholicism. But note that the Vicar refers to himself as "Catholic" and detests the word "Protestant." The rituals of the High Church of England are very close to those of the Roman Catholic Church, but with the difference—to put it in a very simple way—that the Church of England does not recognize the Pope as the representative of Christ on Earth.

CHAPTERS X THROUGH XIV

SUMMARY

Philip is enrolled in the preparatory school attached to King's School at Tercanbury, an institution designed to prepare the boys for the clergy. He is subjected to the usual cruelty of the other boys to a newcomer and finds it doubly difficult because of his club-foot. After a time his deformity ceases to interest the others, but Philip becomes very sensitive about it. He is unable to take part in sports, and this further sets him aside from the others. He does well in his studies, however, and is known as a bit of a grind, something which does not sit too well with his fellow students. At one point the school is seized with religious fervor and all the boys, including Philip, become very devout. He reads in the New Testament that: "...whatsoever ye shall ask in prayer, believing, ye shall receive." He prays that his foot will be healed, and when this does not happen he feels a dull resentment toward people like his uncle, the Vicar, who had told him that mountains could be moved by faith.

COMMENT

The preparatory school of the King's School at Tercanbury would seem a terribly harsh place for a boy of nine today, but apparently it was typical of English public (private) schools of the time. The cruelty that Philip was subjected to by older boys is no different from that which others endure, except that with his club-foot he is forever unable to become one of the crowd and remains an outsider.

While Maugham does not tell us the exact dates, it would appear that Philip spends some three and a half years in the preparatory school. The various incidents during his stay are designed to show how, in this growing-up period, Philip is drawing more and more into himself. Life is a misery, and so, sometimes he feels that he is living in a dream and he will awake in the morning to be with his mother again in London. On one occasion this dreamlike feeling causes him to make up a story about a pen holder which he tells another boy his mother gave him. The boy broke it by accident, and Philip quite suddenly weeps. The story is untrue. He bought the object himself during his last holiday, but the story about how his mother gave it to him before she died makes him so unhappy that he is as sad as if it had been true.

The wave of religiosity that hits the school is made to order for Philip at this time. He finds in it a hope that God will perhaps make him whole if he believes with all his soul. When his uncle tells him that it is true that faith can remove mountains, he prays that his foot will be healed, and he is convinced that God will answer his prayers before the Christmas holidays end. When no miracle occurs, he tells his uncle who explains that it means he "hadn't got faith." Philip cannot understand this; he thinks that no one could have believed more than he did. Finally he comes to the conclusion: "I suppose no one ever has faith enough."

Maugham shows, step by step, that the little orphan is discovering he can depend on nothing but himself. At times he injects a subjective note, but on the whole it is an objective recounting of events that makes the reader realize what a bleak world it is in which Philip is forced to live.

NOTES

Carey
The use of the last name without the prefix "mister" is common in Britain when an older man addresses a younger, or when two males of similar age address each other. The practice is followed in British public schools among the students.

Potted Meats
Deviled ham and the like, called spreads in this country.

Rum
When the boys in the dormitory look at Philip's club-foot, they use this expression. It is British slang for strange or queer, as in "That's a rum situation."

Nibs
This generation may not be aware that there was a time when the fountain pen—or the ballpoint—did not exist, and steel nibs, the writing ends of pens, were inserted in pen holders. They looked much like the nibs on fountain pens today, but came in various sizes and points.

Cane
Corporal punishment in British schools was standard procedure. The cane used was generally a light stick of willow and would be applied to the seat of the pants, or in some cases across the open palm of the hand.

Swat
   Another British slang term meaning study. A swat was a grind, a good student.

Tempter
   The devil or Satan.

Half a Crown
   A silver coin worth two and a half shillings.

Boots
   In Britain these can be what are called boots in this country, but they are also shoes in general.

Baths in Summer
   This does not refer to the ordinary bath, but to bathing.

Exeat
   A temporary absence from school.

CHAPTERS XV THROUGH XXI

SUMMARY

At thirteen, Philip enters the King's School at Tercanbury (as distinguished from the preparatory school). It is an ancient school, dating back to the days of Henry VIII. The curriculum is classic, with emphasis on the dead languages. But shortly before Philip enrolled, a headmaster once a brilliant student at the school, was installed. Mr. Perkins had "new" ideas, and such things as the teaching of French and German were instituted. Philip does well in school in the beginning. In the British public school fashion of the day he becomes attached to a boy named Rose and they are fast friends for a time, but after a while they quarrel and Philip again finds himself alone. Mr. Perkins, who is interested in seeing Philip enter the ministry, takes an interest in him, but when Philip finally shows no inclination to try for a scholarship at Oxford, turns against him. Philip then decides he would like to leave school and go to Germany for a year, an idea that has come into his head because of the experience of another boy who was at King's School and is now in Hanover. He wants to see the world, but his first try at getting away is foiled by the Vicar and Mr. Perkins, who prevail on him to stay at the school a little longer. In the end he wins out but is not sure whether it is a victory or not.

COMMENT

In these chapters Maugham draws for us a picture of a "modest" public school at a time in England when the distinction between the gentry and others was just beginning to break down. He shows us how this school — while not on a par with such famous public schools as Eton, Harrow, or Rugby — was sufficient for the needs of the sons of the local gentry and professional people of Kent. It prepared them for the professions open to gentlemen, with special emphasis on the clergy.

The school is stirred, however, when a new headmaster is appointed who is not a "gentleman," but the son of a tradesman who had attended King's School and later Oxford on scholarships. The other masters (teachers) who have been at the school for years are shocked. They consider resigning but realize in time that this step might be a regretful one.

In this atmosphere Philip at first finds himself more at home than he had before. He does well in his studies, and while he does have a falling out with a stupid master by the name of Gordon, the sympathy that the headmaster, Mr. Perkins, apparently feels for him, makes up for it.

Maugham tells us that Philip passed the first two years with "comfortable monotony." This is the life of a British public school, one that might seem very harsh to an American, but was the accepted thing for a British gentleman of the era. There are descriptions of several masters, all different in their approach to the boys: some tyrants, others easy-going and pleasant.

Two people now affect Philip's life considerably. One is Mr. Perkins, the headmaster, who speaks kindly to Philip when he is smarting under the emotional horror of having been called a cripple by Gordon. For him, Philip develops a "dog-like adoration." Mr. Perkins apparently sees in Philip a brilliant boy who can follow in his own footsteps. Because of the headmaster, some of Philip's early piety, lost when God did not answer his prayers, returns, and he enters into the confirmation ceremony with gladness in his heart.

But, as Maugham points out, Philip could not stay on the heights for long. He still performs his religious exercises, but they are now little more than that. His reading and his solitary habits have also developed in him a somewhat caustic sense of humor. It is this, and his sarcastic ways, which he developed as a defense, that make his dealings with the second person who enters his life at this time significant.

He makes friends with a boy named Rose, the antithesis of all that Philip is. Rose is big and athletic and popular with the other boys — and not too bright. He is a nice boy with a lot of charm, and he takes a liking to Philip — a liking that Philip does not quite know how to handle. For a time they become inseparable friends, but we sense that Philip feels that this is something too good to last. He is not geared to handling the situation. As Maugham in many of his other stories brings out, a man destroys the thing he loves most. Philip begins to feel jealous of Rose's popularity with others; he picks quarrels that Rose cannot understand the reasons for, and in time Rose breaks off the relationship. Philip, in rebellion, takes up with a boy named Sharp, an unpopular "non-gentleman," who is only significant in the story for one reason that will become clear later. On one occasion Rose tries a reconciliation, but Philip, in the manner of those lonely people who feel that any hand put out to them is only in pity, rejects him, thereby antagonizing Rose for good and only adding to Philip's misery.

At about this time Philip loses all interest in his studies. Like many intelligent youths, he finds the routine work distasteful and longs for something else. Mr. Perkins is unhappy at Philip's disinterest, but gets nowhere when he tries to talk to him. While we gather that Philip would like to please Mr. Perkins and agree to try for a scholarship at Oxford and for a life in the clergy, he has come to the conclusion that the life of the vicars he has known is not something he desires. There is a rather cruel description of several vicars in the neighborhood that Maugham may or may not have invented. In his later writings he is not known for gentleness toward men of the cloth. "Rain" is a case in point.

Philip has heard from Sharp, who is in school in Hanover, and this gives Philip the idea that he would like to go to Germany. He feels he can no longer bear the life at Tercanbury. The announcement comes as a shock to his uncle and aunt, and they resist him. Maugham suggests that Philip's going to Germany fell in with some of the new thinking that had been filtering through to the vicarage. In the end they decide that Philip will return to school for another term, and then should leave.

The adults have no intention, however, of letting Philip leave the school, and he discovers that he is the victim of chicanery. He reacts furiously and speaks unkind words to both his uncle and aunt. But his uncle relents again and after Mr. Perkins has spoken to him Philip decides that he can stand another term at school when he knows he will be leaving in the spring for Germany. He finds out, however, that Mr. Perkins had tried to trick him and had no intention of letting him go. But he has his uncle's word, and his uncle controls his finances. Philip leaves the school.

One incident is dismissed in a few paragraphs but is significant in the light of what is to come. His aunt buys him a water-color set and Philip displays a certain natural talent for painting.

In these chapters, Philip passes through the difficult years of puberty into young adulthood. While his sensitiveness and introversion are still apparent, Maugham shows us that Philip is learning to live in this world. He is also learning to fight back, and this takes the form of using his intelligence and wit against those who are normal and not afflicted as he is. This is an ambivalent period when Philip alternately cares and hates, hates and cares. First we find the rather easy life at school, then the difficult, then the good friend and the headmaster, then the break with them, then the hope of the German trip, the letdown and finally the realization of his wishes. It is a see-saw, but even at the end of Chapter XXI, Philip has his doubts.

There is nothing haphazard about the laying-out of these chapters. It is the work of a highly proficient professional writer setting the groundwork for what is to come. Note particularly Philip's relationship with his uncle and aunt. It will become significant later.

NOTES

Conquest
The Norman Conquest of Britain by William in 1066.

Four Professions
The four professions open to a "gentleman" at this time were the agrarian (gentleman-farmer), the military, the church, and the law. It should be noted that farmer meant gentleman farmer, or more correctly a landowner who might or might not supervise the management of his estate. The military, of course, meant a commission in either the Army or the Navy. While the Navy in Britain is the senior service, a commission in the Army was generally considered more aristocratic, particularly in such crack regiments as the Guards, the Buffs, and the Black Watch, to name only a few. These commissions were bought, whereas a commission in the Navy, while also costing money, had to be earned by passing through a rigorous course starting as a midshipman at a tender age. The church—that is to say the Church of England—was another profession open to the gentleman. It was desirable to have money also, for the Church did not pay much, and only those who could keep up their social standing had much chance of advancing to Bishop. Finally, there was the law. But here, too, a distinction was made in Britain between the two classes of lawyers, barristers, and solicitors. The barristers were the gentlemen, although the solicitors may have done most of the work.

The Guardian
Another great British newspaper, the *Manchester Guardian*. It has recently reverted to calling itself *The Guardian*, published in both Manchester and London.

Linendraper
A retail dealer in linen and other cloths.

Magdalen
One of the colleges at Oxford. Pronounced Maudlin. The University referred to in capitals is Oxford.

Wellington and Rugby
Famous public schools.

Chapter

In this sense, a body of the canons and others presiding over the affairs of a church diocese in an area dominated by a cathedral and having jurisdiction over church affairs in the district. The cathedral is presided over by a Dean. Like the famous or infamous "Red Dean of Canterbury."

Form

This is simply a British term for school class.

General Gordon

The gentleman referred to here is the famous "Chinese" Gordon, whose exploits in China and Egypt made him one of the great British heroes of the period.

Construing

A Roman torture every Latin scholar must go through. It consists of translating the Latin text word for word and also going in for declensions such as *femina, feminae feminam,* and so forth.

Gypsy Counter-Jumper

The first word is self-explanatory. Mr. Perkins was dark, and gypsy was a term of opprobrium. The "counter-jumper" refers to a tradesman, or one who will jump over the counter to wait on his customers. Also opprobrious — in this period of British history.

Crib

This is a pony, or published translation of the original Latin work.

Lines

A punishment where one was required to write over and over something like: "I will not talk in class again."

Confirmation

A rite administered to baptized persons in various Christian churches. It is held to convey special grace which strengthens the recipient for the practice of the Christian faith.

Hundred a Year

Again the matter of money comes up. This is the equivalent of $500, and seems like a very small sum, but it was enough to live on quietly and comfortably at the time.

Rot

A British term denoting nonsense. American "nuts."

Blighter

Mild term denoting disrespect of a person. Far more acceptable than others starting with the same letter.

Cockney

This is the true Londoner who drops his "H's" as in " 'orse" for "horse," and so on.

Sixth

The sixth form, the highest grade in British private schools, somewhat equivalent to the 12th grade in the United States, but probably far advanced in liberal arts studies and similar to a student leaving junior college.

Up to Oxford

One went "up" to Oxford, and if expelled from the University or suspended one was sent "down." This expression occurs often in English literature.

Frivolous Ringlets

In the early Victorian years, young ladies wore their hair in a series of ringlets, somewhat like coiled springs down the back of their necks. It was a charming hairdo, depending on your point of view, but apparently looked somewhat silly on an older woman.

Captain of the Eleven

The reference is obviously to cricket, which is played by eleven on a side, although the same is true of soccer or association football. However, the latter is a plebian game, and the football that Philip refers to is probably rugby, which has 15 players on a side.

O.K.S. Match

The annual match in either cricket or rugby between the "old boys" and the regulars. The initials refer to Old King's School.

CHAPTERS XXII THROUGH XXXI

SUMMARY

These are the chapters that deal with Philip's stay in Heidelberg. Through an old friend of the Vicar's Philip learns of a place to live in the house of Professor Erlin, a teacher in the local high school. The family consists of the Professor, his wife, and two grown daughters, Thekla and Anna. Among the boarders are a Chinese and "two or three" Americans, in addition to two German girls. On the first day after a hearty German dinner, several of them go for a walk and when Philip looks down on the Rhine from the heights above the river he tells himself that he is very happy. Philip continues to study—German and Latin from the Professor and French from Monsieur Duroz and mathematics from an Englishman named Wharton, working for a philological degree at Heidelberg University. He leads a pleasant life free from the problems of the King's School. After three months a new boarder, an Englishman named Hayward who is in his middle-twenties, arrives, and in time he and Philip become friends. There is also the American, Weeks, with whom Philip discusses various matters including theology. Hayward is a dilettante who has a fairly comfortable income and flits about Europe, never staying long in one place. He paints for Philip a romantic world that he finds fascinating. Heidelberg begins to look very humdrum, but he does enroll at the University and takes a few courses. However, when his aunt writes to suggest he return to England that summer to talk things over about his future, he is happy to leave.

Maugham is not advancing the main plot in these chapters that tell of Philip's year in Heidelberg, but he is showing that for the first time since his mother's death, Philip is reasonably happy.

The life he describes of a boarding house run by impoverished but genteel folk in a famous German university town is probably typical of a great number of similar *pensions* that existed in continental Europe at the time. The Professor — who is actually a teacher at the local high school — and his wife and his daughters are the prototype of Teutonic middle-class society, but Maugham shows us the difference between the warm, comfortable life they lead and the austere, cold one he was used to in the same social class in England. Here, at least, there are meals that are palatable and substantial, there are beer and wine, and walks with girls to look at the Rhine and good talk and companionship. By present day standards the life is all very innocent but Maugham brings out its *gemutlichkeit* quality.

The various people Philip meets are of no great consequence insofar as the story line is concerned, but he is showing us how a boy of eighteen is being influenced by those he meets. Hayward — the only one who will appear in the story later — the drifter, and Wharton and the Geneva professor and Weeks, the American theological student, are all inserted in the story only to bring out the different types that Philip will eventually meet. They are advancing his education as he grows into adulthood. We are also made to realize that Philip is more and more becoming a spectator of the human foibles that go on around him — and yet the stage is being laid for the time when Philip will become a very active participant in this world.

The story of the Chinese student and the expatriate German girl who both live at the Professor's house, fall in love and eventually run away together to an unknown destination, is strictly a subplot, but Maugham may have inserted it to show how there is no logic in love, and how two completely dissimilar types will be attracted to each other, or one to the other. This is, of course, the central theme of the book and one, incidentally, that Maugham uses in various different ways in many of his later writings.

The contrast between Hayward and Weeks, the serious-minded American theological student from Harvard, is of interest in revealing the manner in which the young Philip reacts to their different characters. Weeks, Maugham shows, is the genuine article, while Hayward is strictly a phony. As Weeks says, he has met a great many of them in Europe, where in Italy he drinks too much wine and in Germany too much beer and always admires the right thing, whatever it happens to be. Philip thinks this is nonsense, and he is attracted by the "worldly" Hayward.

Philip's dealings with Weeks and Hayward, however, do have a profound effect on his faith. As we have seen, Philip has been brought up in a deeply religious atmosphere, and while his piety has been diminished somewhat by God's failure — as he sees it — to cure his lame foot, Philip is still a firm believer. But while he listens to Hayward and Weeks argue about religion, he begins to think deeply about it. He questions Weeks about various aspects of religion, and he questions himself. The result is that he stops believing — or at least thinks he has stopped. He believes that he has become an atheist, and is elated at the discovery. But, as Maugham indicates, it is a rather strange form of atheism, for he says to himself: "If there is a God after all and he punishes me because I honestly don't believe in Him I can't help it."

These chapters, in essence, tell of the first independent awakening of Philip's mind. In Heidelberg he discovers a world he had never known existed. He is exhilarated by it, by the new surroundings, the new freedoms, the new acquaintances, but at the same time he has actually not found anything solid. He thinks that he has grown up, but this is not really the case, and he is simply exchanging one set of rather false values for another. This will be shown as the story progresses.

NOTES

Thirty Marks
The Mark is the German unit of currency. At the time it was worth about 25 U.S. cents.

Pension
Pronounced "ponsyon," a boarding house.

Burschenschaft
German word meaning a fraternity. At Heidelberg these were often dueling fraternities, a strange institution from a non-German point of view, but much admired by the Teutonic even today, although it is now prohibited. In essence, this consisted of a group of students who drank beer together, sang together, and duelled each other with sabres. They were well protected except around the face, and the duel ended when one man was cut. A scar on the face was a mark of honor.

Kneipe

German slang for a place where a group gathered. "Dive" or "hangout" or "pad" would be the American equivalent.

Cheeks Gashed

See the reference to duels above.

Stadtgarden

State garden, a sort of city square.

India-Rubber

This is simply rubber, the raw product. Rubbers in Britain are what we call galoshes. A rubber is an eraser.

Hussar

A cavalry soldier.

Von

Von in German means "of," but the reference here is to such names as Von Hindenberg, Von Rauffenstein, and so forth, which generally indicated that the person was of noble birth as distinguished from such plebian names as Schmidt and Braun.

Ich Liebe Dich

This, as the author explains, means "I love you" in German. This being what might be called a familiar term, the familiar second person singular "you" — dich — is used. The more formal "you" in German is sie, but to say "Ich lieben sie" would be ridiculous.

Faust

This is Goethe's great novel.

War of Seventy

The Franco-Prussian War of 1870 that saw the defeat of France and the beginning of the German Empire.

Prussians

It should be borne in mind that while Germany by now was ruled by the Prussian Hohenzollerns, not all Germans by any means were Prussians. The military was dominated by the warlike northerners, but the more gentle Bavarians and Saxons and Platt Deutsch and others felt that they were the more cultured.

Verruckter Kerl

The author translates this as "madman," but a more apt slang expression might be "crazy nut."

Wagner

It is interesting to note that Wagner, today considered one of Germany's greatest composers, was generally held in contempt by contemporaries because his music at the time was considered revolutionary.

Garibaldi

Guiseppe Garibaldi is considered one of the greatest of Italian patriots. He was one of the founders of modern Italy as a nation. The reference here to his fight against the Pope is in one of his campaigns when he was preparing to enter papal territory around Rome, which in those days was quite considerable.

Commune

After the defeat in the Franco-Prussian War, a Government on communalistic lines was established for a time in France. This is the commune to which Philip refers.

Maibowle

Literally a Maybowl. It is a punch made of wine, spices, and fruit.

Die Wacht Am Rhein

The Watch on the Rhine, Germany's national anthem.

Pater

Walter Pater was an English essayist and critic who was much admired in Victorian times, but like Ruskin and others, he is not very highly regarded today.

Going Over

This indicates conversion to Roman Catholicism from the Church of England.

Pass Degree

There are two types of Bachelor degrees in British universities. An ordinary degree can be secured by doing almost no work at all, so long as the fees are paid. All a "pass" degree means is that the person attended a certain number of lectures, did not get into disciplinary trouble, and stayed at the university for three years. Only an honors or *cum laude* degree means anything scholastically.

Read for the Bar

The bar referred to has nothing to do with an establishment serving alcoholic beverages. The bar is the legal profession, and in Britain to become a lawyer, a person apprentices himself to a law firm and studies in one of the Inns of Court, a legal society which has the exclusive right of admitting persons to the practice of law. The system is a good deal more complicated than can be explained here, but in essence this is the way it works.

Chancery
The British High Court.

Seat
A Seat in the House of Commons. In other words, a Representative in Congress.

Ploughed
Flunked

Briefs
Law cases

Pepper and Salt
A reference to the gray trousers worn at the time.

Waster
The Oxford English Dictionary tells us that a waster is one who lives in idleness. It is unlikely that an American, even at this period, would have used the word. But it is a failing of British authors that they never seem able to make their American characters sound convincing. Maugham is no exception.

Celebrated University
Strange as it may seem today, in many parts of the world, including the former British colonies, there are still only two "celebrated universities," Oxford and Cambridge. In Boston, of course, there is only one.

Damned Yankee
The term, you see, is not new. Today it is "Damn Yankee."

Renan
Ernest Renan was a French philosopher and orientalist. His *"Vie de Jesus"* or "Life of Jesus," is what the title implies, but hardly in accord with the teachings of the Church, for he referred to Jesus as "an incomparable Man."

Dissenters
The other Protestant sects. Not the Church of England.

Chinaman
Maugham uses the term in this book and in some of his works, but it should be noted that most Chinese consider it opprobrious. It is no more acceptable than Jap for Japanese or Wop for Italian.

Mahommedan
Here, too, Maugham is using a term that Muslims (Moslems) do not

like. Mohammed, Mahommed, Mahomet—however it is spelled—was a prophet, but not a god. Allah is the God, and hence worshipped, but not the prophet of the one God.

Collects and Epistles
Collects are short prayers usually concerned with one subject, while an epistle is part of the communion service.

South
The South that Hayward is going to is not our South but southern Europe—specifically Italy.

Hetaira
Loose ladies of ancient Athens. The Anglo-Saxon term is whore.

Moselle
A white Rhine wine.

Bitte
Please, in German.

Gott In Himmel
Literally "God in Heaven," a common German exclamation. It is not offensive, and does not correspond to "My God!" It is more like "For goodness sake!"

Joss-Sticks
Chinese incense in the form of thin sticks.

Bahnhof
Railway station.

Crossing From Flushing
This was before the days of aircraft, and in order to get to Britain, one had to cross the English Channel. Flushing, or Vlissingen, was a port in the Netherlands.

Gemutlichkeit
Maugham does not use this German word but it describes the life in Professor Erlin's home. Literally, the word means "comfortable time," but it is far more than that. *Gemutlichkeit* is a way of life, a feeling, a mood. It takes in such things as beer and sausages and singing and friendships and good discussions, all wrapped up in a hearty German good-eating, good-drinking fellowship of—*gemutlichkeit*.

CHAPTERS XXXII THROUGH XXXV

SUMMARY

These chapters tell of the summer that Philip spends with his uncle and aunt at Blackstable. Also staying at the vicarage is Emily Wilkinson, an Englishwoman who works as a governess in Germany; she was the one who suggested that Philip stay with Professor Erlin in Heidelberg. Miss Wilkinson is a woman of uncertain age, but estimated by the Vicar and his wife to be somewhere between 35 and 40. She has quite a modern way about her, and is very Continental in a fashion quite foreign to Victorian Britain. She flirts with Philip, and as the weeks go by he is attracted to her, although he is aware of the difference in age, and his feelings are more romantically-carnal than romantic. He thinks that it would be a great conquest to have his first affair with her. Before the summer is over this occurs, but Philip is disappointed that it was not the same as the mind picture that he had drawn. Miss Wilkinson demands more and more of him, and by the time she finally leaves for Germany, Philip is much relieved to be rid of her.

In the meantime, after discussions, the Vicar and Philip decide that Philip will enter a chartered accountant's firm in London and learn the business over a period of five years. Philip is looking forward to the "exciting" years to come in London as this episode ends.

COMMENT

The mainstream of the story is not advanced in these chapters, any more than it was in the German episode, but it shows Philip growing up. We hear less of his physical infirmity; he has passed out of the jungle world of children and apparently is less concerned with his club-foot. Maugham tells us that he played tennis rather well, and as will be brought out later, he is quite a good swimmer.

The love story, if it can be called that, is another case of a younger man having his first physical affair with an older woman. Miss Wilkinson, while it may not seem so at first glance, is actually drawn rather sympathetically. Maugham is indicating that she is a creature who cannot escape, however much she may desire it, from the rigid caste lines of Victorian times. Again the question of money arises, and it should be noted that: "Miss Wilkinson was a lady because she was a clergyman's daughter, and a clergyman was a gentleman." When ladies of the period ran into straitened circumstances and were forced to earn a living, there were few courses open. The professions were closed to them, and it was unthinkable to go into trade, which meant working in a store or office. About the only thing they could do was teach. If somewhere along the line the lady had received a musical education and had a Licentiate (degree) from the Royal Academy of Music she could hang out a shingle with L.R.A.M. on it after her name. But if all she had to offer was a knowledge of the three "R's" plus a knowledge of the ladylike requirements of sewing, embroidery, and the like, she probably looked for a position as a governess in a family with means. English governesses were in some demand on the Continent, and one reads about them in other books of the period.

Miss Wilkinson has apparently picked up some rather advanced ideas during her years in France and Germany, but while she is willing to have an affair with Philip, we are led to understand that she places a much greater importance on it than Philip does. To him it is nothing more than an adventure that isn't all he thought it would be. Miss Wilkinson is a forlorn creature, while still maintaining her "lady" ways, she leaves Blackstable and her summer romance. In the field of love, Philip has been the one that scarred his partner. This note of give and take, black and white, has been noted before. Here it is brought into the romantic field. The same theme will continue.

While the romantic interlude is important in Philip's maturing process, it is but another in the incidents that Maugham is inserting to lead into the core of the story. However, none of these are simply incidental. All have a bearing, and again indicate how the polished playwright, in plotting the first of his successful novels (*Liza of Lambeth* was Maugham's first novel, but met with indifferent response) is following a pattern as precise as a blueprint for a ballistic missile.

We learn in these chapters that Philip will go to a chartered accountant's firm to learn the business for five years. While it is indicated that it is not quite the profession for a gentleman, it is becoming more and more acceptable. We will learn more about what the apprenticeship consists of in later chapters.

Finally, while Maugham passes over it again quite lightly, he is preparing us for another aspect in Philip's life. "Why don't you go in for art? You paint so prettily," Miss Wilkinson says at one point. That is about all, but if one recalls that Philip's art ability has been mentioned before, it fits into the pattern that Maugham is weaving.

NOTES

(There is a good deal of French running through these chapters, all of it spoken by Miss Wilkinson. Most of it consists of common phrases and are unimportant to the story itself. The more obscure are translated.)

High Heeled Shoes
The style of the times ran to over-ankle-length shoes, or boots, for ladies, and open-mesh stockings, which were rarely seen by gentlemen.

Heavily Powdered

British ladies did not use makeup in those days. This might be all right for "foreigners" but the only British women who powdered themselves were considered somewhat "fast."

Garden Party

What the name implies. The vicarage apparently had a large garden and a (lawn) tennis court. In England's northern climes — and it should be remembered that if it were not for the warming Gulf Stream Britain's climate would be like that of Moscow — summer twilight lasts for a long time and is the most pleasant time of day.

Button Her Glove

Ladies *always* wore gloves when going outdoors. Winter or summer.

Dog-Cart

A two-wheeled passenger cart that was not pulled by a dog, but a horse. The driver rode looking ahead while the passengers sat on short benches looking outward. It was considered a rather lowly form of transportation.

In a Situation

A situation, differing from a job, was something a lady could take.

Comedie Francaise

Or Theatre Francais, the state theater of France. It was a repertory theater, with a regular cast of actors and actresses, taking different parts as the plays changed. The villain in one might become the hero in another, and so forth.

Deniaser

This is a somewhat vague French term meaning to grow cunning, to lose one's innocence.

Cinquieme

This means fifth in French, but Miss Wilkinson's reference is to the Fifth Quarter of Paris, a poor district. The *ces dames* she refers to are prostitutes, streetwalkers.

C'Etai' Une Fatalite

That is a fatality. Here it probably means "That's fate," however.

Foreigners

This term will come up from time to time. To the British of the day, everyone who was not British was a foreigner. This is understandable, but the term meant a great deal more. Everything that was immoral in their eyes or not quite sanitary was "foreign." Into this category fell spicy foods, perfumes, and even baths. This was British Victorian "logic."

La Vie de Boheme

The story of Bohemian life in Paris by Henri Murger. It was made into a successful play and later in 1898 served as the basis for Puccini's famous opera *La Boheme*.

Invested in Mortgages

Maugham says these paid five per cent, which seems very little for the time. But this was the period of "Pax Britannica" and interest rates were probably down.

Four Professions

The gentlemen's professions come up again, but Mrs. Carey does not list the gentleman farmer and gives the Army as one and the Navy as another.

Chartered Accountant

The profession is similar to that of a Certified Public Accountant (CPA) in the United States, and the charter referred to is a document granting privileges or recognizing rights, like a license to practice.

Articled Pupil

An apprentice, taken in after the signing of articles of apprenticeship; terms of agreement between an apprentice and his employer. Philip is to pay for learning the profession. This system was common in Britain until recently, and may still exist in certain fields.

Practically French

The British seem to feel that the French are obsessed by love, or sex. They are foreigners.

Flannels

When sporting around the tennis courts, British gentlemen wore white flannel trousers. A blazer, a jacket of sometimes startling loudness, was the off-court accompaniment to the flannels.

Swimming Bath

Swimming pool.

Camisole

A woman's undergarment that has blessedly passed into limbo.

Bathing Machine

A curious Victorian device that British (and other, including American) beaches featured. It was a hut on wheels that was rolled into shallow water so that a bather (swimmer) could step into the sea from it without exposing an indecorous amount of "limbs."

Indian Regiment

The young ladies mentioned here are not Indian (Hindu) because their father had been in an Indian regiment. The Indian Army was the British Army on the sub-continent. The regiments were made up of British officers and native enlisted men, and the officers spent their lives of duty in India, returning home every few years for leave. For those gentlemen without considerable private means, it was the only course open if they wished to pursue a career in the Army.

CHAPTERS XXXVI THROUGH XXXIX

SUMMARY

These chapters tell the story of Philip's "exciting" stay in London in the firm of Herbert Carter & Company, chartered accountants. He finds that as an articled clerk he is treated better than the ordinary clerks, but the work is uninteresting and he has no talent for it. He makes no friends, and while he does see a good many plays and goes to the museum and otherwise gets to know the city of London, life in general is a dreary round of going to the office and then returning to his furnished room to read himself to bed. He keeps receiving ardent letters from Miss Wilkinson but finds it hard to answer in kind. He resolves to get away from the life, and this feeling is reinforced when he has a chance to spend a week in Paris with the chief clerk auditing the books of a British hotel. While nothing special happens he is enchanted with the French capital. About this time a letter arrives from Hayward, the dilettante friend he had made in Heidelberg, asking him why he does not go to Paris and study art. Philip is cautious but finally decides he will try to become a painter. He knows that if he leaves at the end of a year, he will salvage half of the sum that has been paid out for his apprenticeship. When he returns to Blackstable he broaches the scheme to the Vicar, who will have nothing to do with it and refuses to give Philip the money he needs to go to Paris. However, unexpectedly, his aunt shows great love for him and exhausts her savings to give him the money.

COMMENTS

Maugham shows us here a picture of life in a British office in Victorian times, an existence that is almost a white-collar serfdom. What is perhaps the most shocking aspect to the present day reader is the strict caste system that prevails. While Philip is called on to do the same kind of menial work that the other clerks do, actually he and the son of a wealthy brewer by the name of Watson, another articled clerk, are the only ones that can ever hope to rise above what they are at present. Even Goodworthy, the managing clerk, is destined forever to remain such.

Here again, we run into the difference between gentlemen and ordinary men in Victorian England. Because Philip was born a gentleman and received a gentleman's education and because he is able to pay the sum of 300 pounds to the firm for his period of apprenticeship, the road is open to him to become a chartered accountant, whereas however brilliant one or another of the other clerks may be, they are destined to stay just that.

Watson, the brewer's son, we gather, is not exactly a gentleman, nor is the head of the company, Mr. Carter. Both are depicted as a new breed that is appearing. Money has made them gentlemen, not birth. We are entering the twentieth century, and even in hidebound Britain, changes are taking place. First in Heidelberg, and now in London, Philip has entered a world that is a far cry from the vicarage and the King's school.

Once or twice there is mention of Philip's club-foot, but this is to keep us reminded of the fact which is a key point throughout the book, and we gather that he is still sensitive but not as deeply as when he was younger.

The exchange of correspondence with Miss Wilkinson has no significance except to show how difficult it is to break off an emotional involvement politely. However, Miss Wilkinson does contribute her bit to Philip's decision to go to Paris and study art by urging him to do so and telling him that he can live in Paris easily on 80 pounds ($400) a year.

Hayward, who will keep on appearing throughout the book, also does his bit in helping Philip make up his mind. His letters are masterpieces of banality, and Maugham fills them with the most ghastly cliches such as "...one should burn with the hard, gem-like flame, one should take risks, one should expose oneself to danger."

The unexpected trip to France is another episode to add to Philip's determination to get away from London.

In Chapter XXXIX we are shown a rather unexpected facet of Mrs. Carey's character. While Maugham has brought out that she truly loves Philip, but is unable to show it, we have been led to believe that she is a good Victorian wife, subservient to her husband in all respects. Here, she rebels. In taking her last savings from the bank and giving them to Philip, she is, in essence, spitting in the Vicar's eye, and this doubly shows the great love she has for her nephew.

Again, while these chapters do not particularly advance the plot line, they show the development of Philip's character, which is actually the whole point of the book. Maugham is demonstrating that life is a series of ups and downs. Philip was anxious to go to London for the "exciting life" then finds that it is not so and is let down, and at the end of this period is "up" again at the prospect of going to Paris.

It should be noted here, in view of what is to come later, that Maugham, the "old pro" writer, has been methodically building up his case against amateurs in the arts. Recall that everyone who has commented on Philip's ability in painting so far has been strictly an amateur. Hayward and Watson and Miss Wilkinson are worthless critics, and Philip's aunt is simply an old woman whose eyes are blinded with love. Maugham does not like those who pretend to know the arts; he despises those who dabble in the arts; and he can be extremely cruel to those who in his opinion have no business doing something for which they are not suited. He makes this point amply clear as the story unfolds.

NOTES

Fourteen Shillings

Again the question of money. Fourteen shillings would be approximately $3.50. For this he apparently also received, in addition to his room, breakfast and tea—or supper, although Maugham does not make this clear.

Tail Coat and Tall Hat

This is a costume seldom seen nowadays except on diplomats at formal daytime occasions. The tail coat is a jacket of sorts with a split back coming down to the knees and curving up in the front. Without the tails it would look much like a present-day suit coat. The tall hat is what we call today a top hat, a shiny, tubular affair. A less glossy variation is still worn by opera goers and men-about-town in New York on very formal occasions.

Desks and High Stools

For some reason or other, the traditional desk of a bookkeeper was a very high affair, and the keeper of the large journals and ledgers sat on a high stool. What advantage this had over an ordinary desk and chair is debatable.

Managing Clerk

What we would call today a chief clerk.

Separate Apartment

In this case, a semi-private office. It shows, however, the difference in caste between the articled clerks and the ordinary clerks.

Hunting

Watson speaks of hunting and shooting, which may seem to be the same thing but are not. Hunting in Britain means fox hunting, or chasing the fox over hill and dale on horseback with a pack of hounds. Shooting is what we call hunting, the killing of deer and birds and other game.

Brewing

This refers to the brewing of beer and ale. It was, of course, a "trade," at this time in Britain, but some brewers, such as the famous Guiness, had made enormous fortunes and broken into the ranks of the "gentlefolk" through sheer force of money. The reference to brewers comes up again and again in Victorian literature and corresponds somewhat to the rich Irish (or other minority group) contractor in America who crashes society because of his wealth. The brewer is depicted as the prototype of a new class that is transforming British social life.

Bounders
Equivalent to "jerk."

Turkey Carpet
What is called a Persian Rug in this country.

Yeomanry
Reserve Army groups. Mr. Carter is obviously a reserve officer in a cavalry unit.

City Man
Only a very small part of the center of London is known as the City — capitalized. Here are the law and accounting and business offices of the metropolis. A City man was a gentleman who worked in these professions; presumably a non-City man was a gentleman farmer.

Fair Copies
Note that Mr. Carter did not believe in typewriting or shorthand; therefore letters had to be copied out in longhand, probably with a steel-nib pen. (The "nibs" in King's School.)

Ruskin
John Ruskin was a noted author and critic of the period, and his views on art kicked up quite a storm at the time. Today he is largely forgotten.

Five Guineas
Philip's evening suit, or what we would call formal wear today, cost him five guineas. A guinea was a gold coin worth 21 shillings. The coin is gone but the term lingers on. Why such a denomination exists only the English know.

Touring Companies
Stage groups that toured the country giving performances in various towns. Quite common in this country until radio and the movies ruined them.

Hook It
British slang for "take off."

Cornwall
Coastal part of Britain, a resort area. A section of the country where noted seamen came from, including Drake and Frobisher.

Squiffy
British slang for drunk, stewed, stoned.

Cockney Accent
This is the famous dropped "H" accent of the Londoner. "Born within sound of the Bow Bells," bells of Bow Church in the center of London. It has other characteristics besides the dropped "H" but "orse" for "horse" is the most well known one. "Aitches" are also added where they are not needed, as in "haddition."

For the Season
Hayward was thinking of coming to London for "the season." This refers to the theater season, and in New York today is still the autumn and early winter months.

Gare du Nord
The North Station, one of Paris' main railroad stations.

Beefsteak Aux Pommes
Beefsteak with potatoes and *vin ordinaire,* the *ordinaire* classifying it as an ordinary or cheap wine.

Thick
British slang for something wicked, exotic.

Only in Paris
This belief, which still persists, is that only in Paris can a budding painter learn his art.

Thirty Francs
About $6.00. The franc, at the time was worth approximately 20 cents based on the gold-backed dollar.

CHAPTERS XL THROUGH LI

SUMMARY

Philip goes to Paris, takes a room in a small hotel in the Montparnasse district, and is thrilled at the thought of living an artist's life. He enrolls in art classes at a studio and makes the acquaintance of, among others, Fanny Price, an Englishwoman of 26, who helps him at first in the mechanics of drawing although it is evident that she has little talent herself. Philip becomes friendly with Clutton, another Englishman who has been in Paris for some time, and who appears to have talent although he wears an air of indifference, and with Lawson, who is a competent but uninspired draftsman. Philip and Lawson eventually take a studio together. The Parisian life agrees with Philip, but it costs him more than he had expected.

Toward the end of this portion of the novel, Fanny Price commits suicide, a victim of hopelessness and abject poverty. After two years Philip decides to face whether he has the talent to pursue an artist's career or not. He has an inherent honesty in these matters and is constantly bothered by what happened to the untalented but stubborn Miss Price. He asks his teacher for a frank opinion and is told he will never be anything but mediocre. It is a blow, but he accepts it, and when he learns that his aunt has died, he leaves Paris and returns to Blackstable.

COMMENT

Philip's two years in Paris are part of the growing-up process, the soul-searching, the quest for identity, that is the core of this semi-autobiographical novel. In themselves, these chapters have no plot advancement, but nothing that Maugham writes is casual. When analyzed in the whole context, every situation has a bearing on the whole.

Fanny Price is presented as the wholly dedicated amateur who believes that with perserverence she can become a professional artist. Her tragedy is in her inability, even when brutally told so, to realize that she has absolutely no talent.

In contrast to Fanny, we have Clutton who is indifferent to criticism, but whom we are led to understand, is probably the only true artist in the group that Philip meets. This does not mean that he will be financially successful, but that nothing should be allowed to interfere with his artistic career.

Lawson, again in contrast, is the future successful artist, the competent draftsman. But unlike Clutton he has no true talent. He is a Miss Price with ability.

Cronshaw, the self-styled poet, is the complete Bohemian, and it is for this reason that the young people admire him even though he is unsuccessful and a drunk. Maugham depicts him as a sort of 20th century Dr. Johnson.

There is a good deal of talk in these pages, what could be called bull sessions. Again, these play a part in the maturing of Philip. Here, one suspects, Maugham is strictly autobiographical, for he indicates that Philip is more and more becoming an observer of man's foibles. Cronshaw, into whose mouth are put the philosophical observations that appear to be Maughams, is not an admirable character, but he certainly reflects Maugham's views if his later works are any indication.

We gather that Fanny Price, in her strange way, has fallen in love with Philip. But she is unattractive and Philip is repelled by her. Her suicide is a shock to him, but only because it is a raw slice of death he is witnessing and not because it affects him personally.

It should be noted, however, that Fanny Price, like Miss Wilkinson, loves Philip but does not receive love in return. Maugham is constantly stressing this theme—that love is very often one-sided. So far Philip has not been the victim but the victimizer.

The character of Fanny Price is of interest when viewed in the light of what is to come. Fanny is shallow, vituperative, unpleasant, and coarse. Note the similarity to another girl Philip will meet later.

Finally, Maugham dwells on the tragedy of those who pursue the arts without having the talent to make anything of their chosen careers. Maugham is, in a sense, sympathetic, but at the same time blunt in his rejection of the mediocre. This is a theme that occurs often in Maugham's works. The old pro has no use for the amateur who masquerades as a creative artist. One suspects that he has a certain admiration for the craftsman with limited talent but only if he works very hard at his craft. On the other hand he has immense admiration for the truly talented even if the individual is a scoundrel. In *The Moon and Sixpence* this is quite apparent. Clutton is a case in point.

While Philip is obviously disappointed to discover he has little talent, we are led to believe that he is not crushed and his stay in Paris has been on the whole a pleasant experience.

We are now about to enter the mainstream of the story. The master playwright has set the stage, and by now the reader should have a pretty good idea of the character of the rootless, crippled orphan who is searching for a place in the scheme of things.

NOTES

Carriage
A railroad passenger car.

Massiere
Someone in charge of a studio.

Latin Quarter
The Left Bank of the Seine River, the Montmarte and Montparnasse section of Paris where the poor artists lived—and still do. It is also a working man's section and not necessarily exclusive to artists.

Charcoal
A fine grade of hardwood charcoal is used by artists for sketching.

Absinthe

A liquor that has a taste like licorice. It was supposed to be the drink of the artist, and because of its narcotic quality, has now been banned. Pernod and Herbisant are Absinthe substitutes with the same taste but without the wormwood.

Pompiers

Literally a pumpman, a fireman. Conventional, stereotyped art.

Turns

The different acts performed in a vaudeville show.

Acetylene

Carbide gas that lights lamps. Still in use in night street construction work.

Pile of Saucers

In Paris cafes the usual practice is to bring a drink and a small saucer. Later, the number of saucers indicate the number of drinks that were consumed.

Test Match

A major cricket series, usually between two countries such as England and Australia. A sort of World Series of cricket.

Il Est Impayable

It is priceless — funny.

Fichez Mois Le Paix

Give me a bit of peace.

Tas de Farceurs

Lot of jokers.

Sale Bete

Dirty dog.

Crapule, Canaille

Debaucher, scum.

Bonne a Tout Faire

Maid of all work.

Funk It

British slang for chicken out.

Dejuener 1-25, Vin Compris

Lunch, 1.25 Francs, with wine.

Stockbroker
The reference to the stockbroker turned artist is obviously meant to be Gauguin, around whose life Maugham later wrote a novel, *The Moon and Sixpence*.

Caporal
Very strong French tobacco.

Garsons de Cafe
Boys of the cafe. Waiters.

Mrs. Grundy
The personification of conventional propriety.

Epicurus
This Greek philosopher defined philosophy as the art of making life happy, with pleasure as the highest and only good.

Levantine
Middle Eastern types from the region of what is today Lebanon. Their ancestors were the legendary trading Phoenicians.

Tarbouch
Can also be spelled "tarboosh," a rimless, stovepipe sort of cap with a tassel. Called "fez" in Turkey.

Roses of Hafiz
Hafiz was a Persian lyric poet, known for his love poems.

Wine Cup of Omar
No educated Victorian was unaware of the Fitzgerald translation of the "Rubaiyat" of Omar Khayyam, the Persian poet-astronomer. Omar believed in wine, women and song.

> "A book of Verses underneath the Bough
> A jug of Wine, a Loaf of Bread — and Thou
> Beside me singing in the Wilderness —
> Oh, Wilderness were Paradise enow!"

Pyjamas
British spelling for pajamas.

Royal Academy
The august British institution of the arts. An R.A. after a painter's name meant he had joined the inner circle. The academy was noted for its conservatism.

Salon
A place where paintings were displayed. In this case it means a place where unknowns could submit their works in the hope of having them hung — displayed.

43

Baedeker
Famous guidebook to all the important places in Europe. Still available.

The Gioconda
The Mona Lisa, by Leonardo da Vinci.

Portmanteux
Trunks, handbags.

Pot-Au-Feu
Literally a "pot of fire," a soup.

Fromage de Brie
Brie Cheese, a creamy type.

Fiasche of Chianti
Wicker-covered bottle of chianti, an Italian wine.

Rabelaisian Figure
A hearty, somewhat vulgar type.

Bourgeoise
The respectable middleclass. The allusion to Mrs. Warren and the profession is to a madam, the proprietoress of a brothel.

Petite Amie
Small friend, a girl friend.

C'est de Votre Age
It is your age (period, time).

Cremerie
Milk shop, small, inexpensive restaurant.

Bureau
Police station.

On the Razzle
British slang for going on a binge, doing the town.

Cheek
An unlikely word for an American to use. Means gall.

Other Side of the River
The Right Bank of the Seine where the better-off and more respectable people lived. The opposite of the "other side of the tracks."

A.R.A.
Associate of the Royal Academy. Not quite as good as R.A., but still a high honor in British artistic circles.

Cenacle
Artistic group or circle.

Pas Mal
Not bad.

CHAPTERS LII THROUGH LV

SUMMARY

Philip returns to England to attend the funeral of his aunt and to stay with his uncle for a time. Realizing that he is not cut out to be an artist, he decides to follow in the steps of his dead father and take up the study of medicine. Because he has had an adequate preparatory education, he is accepted as a student at St. Luke's (hospital), where his father had studied. He goes to London, gets himself rooms near the hospital and takes up his studies. These consist largely of anatomy and dissection, and while he finds the first tedious and the second somewhat unpleasant, he manages to fit into the life of a medical student. He becomes casually friendly with another student named Dunsford, and they often go to plays together. He also makes the acquaintance of another medical student, senior to him, who lives in the same building, an extrovert-type named Griffiths. With Dunsford he goes to a tea shop where there is a waitress named Mildred that Dunsford is momentarily stricken with, but Philip finds her unattractive. She is thin and anaemic and flat-chested. But while Dunsford decides that Mildred is not for him, Philip finds himself going back to the same tea shop, although Mildred largely ignores him.

COMMENT

Philip's return to the vicarage for the funeral of his aunt gives Maugham the opportunity to indulge in a bit of ironic comment on human nature — a characteristic of almost all his works.

Philip is fully prepared to find his uncle brokenhearted. Instead he discovers that the Vicar appears to be far more interested in the trappings of the funeral than in the death itself. On the one hand Maugham is showing what an old hypocrite the Vicar is, but he is also taking a dig at people in general, and possibly illustrating a profound truth. After the Vicar and the church-warden get into a slight argument about the inscription that should be on Mrs. Carey's gravestone, Philip goes out into the garden to smoke and "suddenly began to laugh hysterically." In a sense he is laughing at himself for having been so naive, but at the same time he is also wryly commenting on the strange human animal.

This disillusionment fits in with Philip's acceptance that he has no future as a painter. We see how Philip over the years has become, more and more, a keen observer of his fellow men and in a lesser sense, an observer of himself. This is Maugham the autobiographer talking.

Philip's decision to study medicine is not a well thought out one but more in the nature of a rebuff to his uncle who suggests the course.

In a short subjective interlude we are given a bit of Philip's philosophy of life at this period in his development. He is, as noted before, a "loner" who thinks that he has learned to view the world from outside himself. But he realizes that because of his deformity and his miserable early years, he is still touched by unexpected kindnesses. There follow several pages of Philip's views on life in general, which might be summed up in his statement: "He saw that nothing was good and nothing was evil; things were merely adapted to an end."

Medical school in Britain at this time was considerably different from the curriculum we have today in this country. The schools, if they could be called that, were attached to hospitals, and if the candidate had a sufficient educational background in Latin and the liberal arts in general, he was assumed to be capable of becoming a doctor if he studied hard and could pass the periodic examinations. Maugham explains the system in some detail as he goes along and it should be fairly clear. This teaching method of lectures and examinations at specific times, is still characteristic of British higher education.

Philip now meets the person who is to have a profound effect on his life. This relationship is the main theme of the novel.

It has been noted previously that the book is a study in ambivalence. Nothing is all good; nothing is all bad. Philip has loved and hated, been happy and sad.

Now Philip meets Mildred, the tearoom waitress. At first he is disinterested, thinks her unattractive and only speaks to her to try and help out his friend Dunsford who is very shy with women. When he is rebuffed Philip is angered. But he returns to the tearoom and he begins to think about Mildred.

We are about to enter the mainstream of the story. Maugham will bring out as he goes along all the various facets of Mildred's character, but the first impression that Philip has should be kept in mind. Maugham remains objective so that the reader's impression should approximate Philip's.

NOTES

Squire
   In this context a landed country gentleman with money.

Dissenting Minister
   Any churchman not of the Church of England.

Coom's Tickets
   Thomas Cook & Son is a travel agent firm. The term "Cook's tour" derives from the name of the company: a guided tour.

Mr. Cameron
   Mister was and is a surgeon in Britain. Doctors are doctors of internal medicine.

Dado
   The lower part of an interior wall different from the upper part.

Scone
   A biscuit, or a close cousin of the American species.

Conjoint
   Combined. (The system of medical education is explained at some length in the novel.)

F.R.C.S.
   Fellow of the Royal College of Surgeons.

Ripping
   British slang for good or happy, as in a "ripping time."

P.M. Room
   Post mortem room. Where the autopsies are held.

Apothecaries Hall
   Where druggists—the British call them chemists—were trained.

Harley Street
   Fashionable address for society doctors in London. A "Harley Street physician" is an expensive, and presumably crack doctor.

Alexandra Fringe
   Bangs named after Queen Alexandra, the consort of Edward VII, King at the time.

Sacked
   Fired, dismissed from employment.

CHAPTERS LVI THROUGH LXII

SUMMARY:

Philip feels humiliated at the way in which he has been snubbed by Mildred, and he begins to go to the tea shop daily, in order, he tells himself, to wipe out the humiliation. But when Mildred finally speaks a few words to him, he is elated, and when one evening he does a sketch of her, she seems quite friendly. But the next day she is cool to him again, and spends her time talking to a German who appears to be her boy friend. When he eventually asks her to go to a musical comedy with him, she accepts. The evening is not particularly enjoyable to Philip, but he realizes that for some reason he cannot explain, he has fallen in love. Mildred is indifferent to his feelings, but occasionally throws him a small scrap of affection. Philip is unhappy and humiliated at his own feelings, but he cannot stay away from her. He knows she is seeing the German and he is consumed by jealousy. His studies are neglected, but he is so obsessed by Mildred that he cannot concentrate on them. For a while he manages to stay away from the tea shop, but after he fails his first examination in biology, he can no longer restrain himself and returns. He is again humbled, but when she consents to go out with him he is overjoyed. When she allows him to kiss her, his joy knows no bounds. They now dine together once or twice a week and he gives her presents that he can ill afford. But they quarrel, because of her indifference, and because of his passion, and each time they make up it is only because Mildred tolerates it. Finally, although he knows it is folly, he asks her to marry him, but after she questions him on his finances she coolly refuses him.

COMMENT

Here we enter the main body of the plot. Everything that has gone before is strictly secondary, and between Chapter LVI and the end of Chapter CIX, there is a novel within a novel, which could stand by itself as a fine work.

The physical description that Maugham gives of Mildred is definitely not attractive. She is flat-chested, tall and thin, with thin lips and an anemic look. But she apparently has fairly good looking features, and men are attracted to her. The German is an example, and he will play a part in the story later.

Here we are again running into the ambivalence that runs through the whole book. Philip, for the first time, falls in love, desperately and hope-lessly, with a woman who cares not a whit for him except possibly for what little he is able to give her monetarily. She treats him in the most abom-inable manner, but Philip keeps coming back for more and more abuse. He is objective enough at times to realize that he is only making a fool of himself, but objective thinking has no place in the passion he feels.

We know enough of Philip by now to realize that he is a sensitive, lonely, kindly person, and in many ways an admirable one although irresolute so far. He is now in the clutches of a scheming, calculating, heartless woman, who will use him only for what she can get out of him. But the shackles are made by Philip. At this stage, Mildred is completely indifferent and would let Philip go at any time he wishes.

The reader's sympathy must be for Philip, and the question can be asked why he puts up with the abuse he receives from this slut. Maugham's answer, one that he will develop as he goes along, is the one contained in the title. What makes a person a slave?

By the end of Chapter LXII, Philip is thoroughly hooked. He has done everything to try and win her, even for a night. He has appealed to her sympathy, mentioning his club-foot, a humiliation he has never subjected himself to before; he has offered to kiss the ground she walks on; he has offered her a trip to Paris he cannot afford. And finally, he asks her to marry him, although he knows this is complete folly.

Again and again there is the ambivalence, the love and hate that Maugham sees in love. Philip loves her madly, senselessly, but at the same time he wants to hurt her for the suffering she has caused him. And Maugham indicates that this is impossible, for you can only be hurt if you love.

NOTES

Sixpenny Reprints
What we call paperbacks today.

Stick
Gentlemen of the day generally carried a walking cane.

Waiting Rooms
Railroad trains had classes: first, second and third, and so did waiting rooms in stations. Nothing was integrated between the classes in Victorian days.

Going It
British slang for "Putting on the dog."

Fiz
Fizz water, slang for champagne.

Stick Her
Slang for "stand her."

Eastbourne
Seaside resort for the "lower middle" class.

West-End People

Better part of London, contrasted to the East-End, the slums and Soho, a "foreign" district.

Season

Season ticket.

Odiously Genteel

This will come up many times in reference to Mildred's manners and habits. It was true, at the time, that many of the uneducated lower class, and particularly the women, would try to ape the ways of what they thought were those of the gentlefolk.

Offence

If your edition spells it this way, it is not an error. The British often use "c" in words we spell with "s," such as defence for defense.

Hansom

Maugham himself comments on the advantages of this vehicle, a two-wheeled carriage where the driver sat up more-or-less on the roof.

Aunt's Queer

Queer in this sense means that her aunt is not feeling well.

Music Hall

A vaudeville theater of the kind that used to exist in the United States. Certain shows on television featuring dancers, singers, dog acts, and ventriloquists, will give an approximation of what transpired.

Viva

An oral examination.

Idealisation

If this is the spelling in your book, it is again not an error. British often use "s" instead of "z."

A.B.C. Shop

A well-known chain of reasonable restaurants or tea shops in London.

Ploughed

Flunked.

The Embankment

Road by the Thames River.

Soho

A foreign section of London known for its cheap French and Italian restaurants, among other things. Also, supposed to be a den of vice.

Commercial Traveller
A traveling salesman.

Japanese Print
The woodblock prints of such artists as Hiroshige, Utamaro, and Hokusai, that influenced the French impressionists with their bold style.

CHAPTERS LXIII THROUGH LXVIII

SUMMARY

Philip now changes his tactics toward Mildred. He does everything he can to be nice to her and avoids quarrels, listens patiently to her silly prattle and becomes her confidante. There is no indication that she is returning his passion, but she begins to show some signs of affection. Philip is delighted; then quite suddenly she tells him that she is going to marry Miller, the German. Philip is stunned and saddened and decides that he will see no more of her. The arrival of his old Heidelberg friend, Hayward, and the meeting with the painter Lawson at an art gallery, helps Philip to put Mildred out of his mind somewhat. He begins to feel like a patient recovering from a bad illness. Through Lawson he meets a young woman, Norah Nesbit, who is separated from her husband and making a precarious living writing pot-boilers. Norah is cheerful and gay and witty and all the things that Mildred was not. While Philip does not fall in love with her, he likes her very much, while she, on her part, falls in love with him. They enter into an affair that is apparently pleasing to both of them. Philip passes the two examinations he had previously failed plus a third one and is now well on his way. At a tavern one night with Lawson and Hayward he meets a stockbroker named Macalister, who tells him of the fortunes that could be made in stocks. Philip looks forward to a tip that will bring him in some money so that he can buy Norah some things she needs.

COMMENT

These are the chapters that might be called the First Emancipation of Philip. After Mildred tells him that she is going to marry Miller, he makes a physical break with her, although he suffers emotionally.

The past, in the form of his Heidelberg and Paris sojourns, now comes to his aid. The first medicine for his emotional wounds is Hayward, whose conversation, while not the most intellectual in the world, is still a far cry from the nonsense he has been subjected to by Mildred for a long time. The meeting with Lawson adds to the therapy, and Philip is transported back to his days in Paris which he can now view in the bright light of hindsight. We are led to believe that he has shaken off the Mildred shackles; Maugham tells us that his work is going easily and he is studying hard to make up for the two exams he had flunked.

The entry of Norah into his life completes the cure, or so one would think. Norah is a delightful character, completely different from Mildred. Norah is intelligent and charming and honest and completely without airs of any sort, all characteristics that were sadly lacking in Mildred. The affair that she has with Philip is depicted as a healthy, satisfying one both physically and emotionally. Both of them are happy.

But note that there is one catch to this relationship. Again Maugham is bringing out the ambivalence of love, of the bondage of one individual to another. Norah is in love with Philip but Philip is not in love with Norah. He is grateful to her for her kindness, for the love she gives him, for the sympathy she shows when he tells her of his experience with Mildred, and for her feelings about his deformity. He is grateful—and this word is used many times—but he is not in love. Again, the playwright is setting the stage. The word will come up later in the story in a very different way.

This is a happy period for Philip. He has found himself a good companion, a wonderful woman, and he is pursuing his chosen career. When he passes his exams and thus delights Norah, he is at about as high a point as he has been in his life so far. But keep in mind the see-saw nature of the book.

There is one minor incident—at this point—that will have a bearing later. This is Philip's meeting with the stockbroker Macalister.

There is in these chapters a good deal of philosophical talk, which has no bearing on the story as such, but again shows us that Philip is becoming more and more a keen observer of the moving scene. Hayward is the butt now of Philip's barbs. While once, in Heidelberg, he listened in wonderment to what the dilettante spewed forth, he is now the skeptic who takes nothing that Hayward says as anything more than banalities. At one point, when Hayward says that something would have interfered with his work, Philip asks: "What work?" At the same time, Philip is obviously fond of Hayward and Lawson, and he enjoys talk, the talk of the young.

Toward the end of these chapters, Philip catches influenza, and quite unexpectedly, is nursed carefully by Griffiths, the sophisticated medical student that lives above him in his lodgings. Griffiths takes great pains to help Philip recover. Philip is puzzled and pleased.

This again, is a scene setter. Maugham never forgets his playwright's training. It should be evident by now, and will become more so as the story progresses, that every segment of the plot has been carefully arranged to fit on to the next.

NOTES

Number Was Up
This is not the common meaning of the expression. Apparently, names of those who passed were put on a board.

Sunday on the River
Picnics in small boats on the Thames, a favorite summer relaxation of Londoners.

Patronne
The owner of the restaurant.

Lady Smoking
This was in Victorian times and only "wicked" women smoked in public. What they did in private is another matter, and there are indications that many a duchess enjoyed a cigar or two.

Registry Office
A civil marriage is referred to here, and it has some bearing on what is to come.

Dressing Bag
A woman's handbag, containing a mirror, brushes, and other paraphernalia for making-up. Incidentally, 20 pounds or $100 was a great deal of money for such an object.

Penny Steamboat
Public steamers that go up and down the Thames carrying excursionists.

Siam
The name is Thailand today.

Inigo Jones
Noted British architect of the 17th century.

Rotter
Somewhat stronger than "bounder," but both meaning a person out of the mainstream, a bad egg.

In to Tea
A polite way of saying that she would be at home and welcoming visitors.

Penny Novelettes
Love, adventure or detective stories put out in cheap editions.

Supers
Walk-on actors who take bit parts or simply hold a spear.

Ripper
Somewhat like a rip-snorter, but in this case indicating a wonderful person.

Linen
The reference here is to his shirts—the sewing-on of buttons and so forth.

End Up
Chin up.

Out Patient's Clerk
Somewhat along the lines of an intern on outside duty—ambulances and the like.

Bad Light
Artists are very sensitive about the light in which they paint. London in winter has practically no light at all.

Reading
The comment that Maugham has Philip make here about the habit of reading is one he brings up often in his other writings: that once you have gotten the habit you can no more drop it than any other habit.

Rum Punch
Maugham's rapturous description should give some idea of its qualities. It is made of rum and other ingredients, differing from place to place.

Seedy
Not well.

Siphon
The meaning here is obscure, but could mean a drinking tube made of glass so that Philip can sip drinks while lying down.

Lark
A pleasant experience.

Furs
Ladies of the period word various things made of fur, such as collars, stoles and muffs, the latter a sort of fur roll into which both hands were put. Fur coats as such were not common.

CHAPTERS LXIX THROUGH LXXII

SUMMARY

Philip returns home one day to find that Mildred is waiting for him. Once again, the passion and love that he had thought he no longer had, returns. It seems that Mildred was never married to Miller, and when he found she was pregnant, he deserted her. Philip loves her more than ever, for now he feels sorry for her. He gives her money and finds her lodgings and arranges for her to have the baby in a nursing home. In the meantime, he breaks with Norah, although in the beginning he tries to maintain a friendly relationship. But in the end he is cruel to her and Norah is heartbroken. Philip is completely wrapped up in Mildred, and although he is shocked to find that she neither wants to have the baby nor to take care of it after its birth, he is the one who pays for everything and looks after the details. Mildred has a baby girl without any complications. Philip arranges to send her to the seashore for a couple of weeks and after that they are to go to Paris together.

COMMENT

The brief emancipation is over and Philip is hooked again. This time it is even worse, for now he is not only senselessly in love with her, but he feels sorry for her and therefore wants to do things for her.

The break-up with Norah is another example Maugham gives of how much easier it is to enter into a love affair than to get out of it. Philip is essentially a kind person and he does not wish to hurt Norah, but as explained earlier, he has never been in love with her and once Mildred has again entered his life he has no room in it for anyone else.

There is nothing unusual in the sad story that Mildred tells Philip about her "marriage" to Miller. But it is a further amplification of the character—or lack of character—of the cold, common, grasping person that is Mildred. When she tells Philip that she wished she had married him, she is not indicating any love for him, but simply that she had played the wrong card. The fact that Philip is pleased at the remark only shows how far gone he is.

In throwing over Norah, in taking up with a pregnant Mildred this time, Philip is divorcing himself from the happiness that he had in the brief interlude between the time he last saw her and now; he is also sowing the seeds of his own destruction emotionally and financially, for we are led to believe that he is living far beyond his means.

Mildred, who is afraid of having the baby, clings emotionally to Philip, although she is not giving him anything. Philip is her crutch, but she gives nothing in return, and takes his money and his kindness as her normal due.

Mildred's attitude toward the coming baby is another indication of the shallowness and selfishness of her character. She has no desire to have it, and indicates that she wishes it would be still-born. Philip is shocked by her attitude, but he is so consumed with love that he can only think of how wonderful it is that she is going to have a child. Maugham is portraying a man in the throes of self-sacrifice, and while he does not say so, he hints that this is a most dangerous emotional situation.

These chapters are fertile fields for the cynic's seeds, but Maugham is not drawing any conclusions. He tells the story, and the reader can draw his own conclusions.

Still again, and again, as the story has progressed, and will progress, we have the see-saw, the happiness and sorrow, the love and hate. Ambivalence, while overused perhaps, is the word.

NOTES

Last Monday Week
British way of saying "a week ago Monday."

Telegram
At this time, when telephones in private homes were rare, the telegram was used quite often. In London, it was, and is, very efficient. They can be sent from any local post office.

Waistcoat
A vest.

Public House
A "Pub" or bar.

Brass Farthing
The farthing was the lowest form of currency, worth a half penny.

Tenner
Ten pounds or $50.

Bant
Go on a reducing diet

Nipping
Some more British slang meaning wonderful.

Undo Me Behind
Women wore corsets in these days and apparently had trouble getting out of them.

Sweet
British term for dessert.

Amours
Love affairs.

Cross
Angry.

Spoil the Ship
Spoil the ship for a coat of tar means simply that there is no point in skimping a few pennies to do a good job.

The Flying Dutchmen
There is a double meaning here. The "Flying Dutchman" is the famous ghost ship of the seas that is supposed to be seen by sailors on occasion. The "Flying Dutchman" Philip refers to is also the flying German, Miller, the Dutchman.

CHAPTERS LXXIII THROUGH LXXVIII

SUMMARY

Three weeks after the birth of the baby, Philip sends Mildred to Brighton, a seaside resort, for a rest. She does not wish to keep the baby and plans to pay someone to look after it. By the time Philip visits her in Brighton, Mildred has found the wife of a curate to take the baby for a few shillings a week. Philip's great joy now is that Mildred has agreed to go with him to Paris, and here he feels that at last his desires will be satisfied. One night, he feels that it would be pleasant if he should introduce Mildred to his friend Griffiths. The three of them have dinner together, and the result is that the handsome and charming Griffiths and Mildred develop a passion for each other. Philip is furious, but he is so immersed in self-torture that he even offers to pay the money so that Griffiths and Mildred can spend a weekend together, if she will promise to return to him afterward. Mildred says she will, and torn as he is by jealousy, Philip gives her the money. Mildred never does return, and when Philip goes to her lodgings day after day, he finally hears that she has taken her things and moved away. He goes to Blackstable for the holidays and while there, does some soul-searching, realizing that physical love is completely irrational, and that the love he has held for Mildred is a hopeless thing unless it is returned — and he realizes that will never happen.

COMMENT

In these chapters Philip reaches the lowest depths of humiliation in his dealings with Mildred. This is the nadir of his self-torture, the inability to escape from the obsession that has possessed him for so long.

Philip is looking after Mildred and her baby by Miller, and without this help she would be helpless. But she takes the attention as her due, and her only concession is to agree that she will go to Paris with Philip, something she would like to do in any case, and the physical favor she will do Philip is in her mind simply that, a full payment for services received.

When Mildred returns to London there are but six days to go before the Paris trip. Philip is very happy, and in his happiness, he decides to share it with Griffiths.

We have been prepared for the Griffiths-Mildred meeting by prior descriptions of Griffiths' character. Maugham always sets the stage, and no character in this novel ever enters it without having some part to play in the future. Griffiths has been shown as a shallow but charming and entertaining fellow, handsome and wellbuilt, of a type that Mildred likes. The results are inevitable.

When Philip learns of the infatuation they have for each other he attempts a break, but Mildred, for financial reasons, is not to be put off so easily. She has learnt that Griffiths does not have any money at all, and she is still dependent on Philip. She comes to Philip and tells him she is ready to go with him to Paris.

When Mildred breaks down and cries, however, because she is not in a position to continue her affair with Griffiths on account of the money angle, Philip is moved to sympathy. He realizes that Mildred, in her own way, is a victim of passion as he is, a passion he had never thought her capable of before.

Philip now deliberately debases himself by offering to pay for Griffiths and Mildred to go away to Oxford for a weekend. He is tortured at the thought, but it gives him a perverse kind of pleasure to be the instrument that will make it possible for Mildred to be with her lover.

The ambivalence mentioned many times before is very evident here. Now the hate and love is within Philip himself. He is not sure why he behaves in this way, although there is a hope that once Mildred has purged herself of this infatuation she will finally come to him.

Mildred takes his money and leaves with Griffiths for Oxford. This is, in a sense, a turning point in the book. Philip is still in love, still consumed with jealousy, still longing for any little favor, but this is the lowest point he can reach. He has paid out money that he can ill afford so as to make it possible for the woman he loves desperately to have an affair with a man he considered his friend. The flagellation is almost unendurable and Philip even contemplates suicide.

When Mildred does not look him up after returning from Oxford, and disappears into the vast London scene, Philip returns to Blackstable for the holidays. He still thinks of her all the time, but we now have him doing a bit of soul-searching, and here his past experiences in human relations make him begin to look at things more rationally. A passage of particular interest that could be said to sum up much of Maugham's philosophy as displayed in many of his other works is when Philip tells himself that in trying to make Mildred love him he had been attempting the impossible.

> He did not know what it was that passed from a man to a woman, from a woman to a man, and made one of them a slave: it was convenient to call it the sexual instinct; but if it was no more than that, he did not understand why it should occasion so vehement an attraction to one person rather than another.

Nonetheless, Philip is beginning to understand. The malady is still there, but the crisis has been passed. The convalescence will be painful, and the prognosis is still not completely positive, but the second emancipation is nearing.

NOTES

Brighton
Brighton is a middle-class seaside resort, a sort of combination of Coney Island and Atlantic City. It has a boardwalk and various concessions and generally chilly swimming in the English Channel.

Lady-Friend
Maugham deliberately uses the term to show Mildred's pseudo-genteelism. No lady of the time would have said anything but "friend," qualifying it by saying "Mrs. Jones" or something of the sort.

Boa
Women of Mildred's class wore long neckpieces made of everything from rabbit to monkey fur. The imitation swansdown was something that looked like swan's feathers.

Cheek
Nerve, as in "what nerve!"

Dr. Brighton or London-by-the-Sea
Brighton was supposed to be therapeutic.

Astrakhan Collar
Persian lamb fur.

Locums
Temporary work.

Aigrette
A feather headpiece that women of the period wore.

Blaud's Pills
Tonic pills, like vitamin pills today.

Two Bob
Two shillings.

Fiver
Five pound note, or $25.

Chimney-Piece
Mantle-piece.

Cure
A card, a comic.

Tall-Boy
A closet or locker.

CHAPTERS LXXIX THROUGH LXXXVI

SUMMARY

Philip returns to London and gets himself an unfurnished apartment. He invites Lawson and Hayward to a housewarming party and Lawson tells him that he had seen Norah recently and she had asked about Philip. This reminds him of how happy he had been with Norah, and he decides to visit her and throw himself on her mercy. Norah receives him kindly, but she has a man taking tea with her. He leaves, and afterward, Philip pours out the story of his life with Mildred. Norah listens sympathetically but tells him that she is engaged to be married. Philip realizes that the gods have played a joke on him. Philip continues his studies, and from a friend of Griffiths he hears that Mildred had made a pest of herself to Griffiths so that he was finally forced to tell her to take off. In time, Philip becomes an out-patients' clerk, something less than an intern, but more than a mere theoretical medical student. He finds that dealing with patients in the clinic is interesting and feels that perhaps he is cut out to be a doctor. There is a brief interlude when he again meets Cronshaw, the poet he knew in Paris; Cronshaw is old and dying, but quite ready to go, regretting nothing. When Philip finds that the old poet is living in terrible circumstances, he prevails upon him to come and live with him, and Cronshaw is happy to do so. He is pleased that his first published book of poems is coming out next spring, and although he knows that if he keeps on drinking he will die, he refuses to give up what he calls his last pleasure.

Cronshaw dies, and Philip arranges for the funeral, another added expense that eats into his now very meager funds. While working in the hospital, Philip meets a patient, Thorpe Athelny, a journalist. They become friendly, for Athelny is a well-educated man, and Philip finds him most interesting.

COMMENT

Philip gets his comeuppance when he tries to take up with Norah again, and while the break on Norah's part is in keeping with her kindly character, it is nevertheless a clean break. Maugham shows us that you cannot break a heart and expect to repair it again at will. At the same time, he reinforces again the somewhat cynical character of Philip that he has been drawing throughout the book. Philip by now has the "gift of being amused at one's own absurdity," and finds it an uncomfortable thing.

The hospital life that Maugham depicts has no main bearing on the story, but does suggest Philip's interest in his fellow men; Maugham is developing—as he has been doing all along—a further sense of objectivity. Philip feels that he is perhaps cut out to be a doctor, and we gather that he is happy that at last he may have found the right profession.

Philip cannot entirely rid himself of Mildred's memory, for Griffiths' friend tells him of their affair, but it again repeats Maugham's premise that love in general is one-sided. Griffiths has no use for Mildred; Mildred is madly in love with him. The contrast to Philip is obvious.

The Cronshaw episode is simply an amplification of Maugham's detestation of phony artists. Not Cronshaw himself, for Maugham admires types who will go down courageously, however wrong they may be, and in depicting an unregenerate drunk who would rather die than give up drinking, Maugham is praising rather than censuring. But he brings in another character, the critic Leonard Upjohn, a type that Maugham abhors. It is apparent that Maugham has met more than his share of the ilk, and he takes delight in tearing them apart. Note the complete artificiality of the man in the matter of Cronshaw's funeral.

The incident where Philip is asked by the surgeon to show his club-foot to the other surgical students is to demonstrate that Philip is still highly sensitive about his deformity.

So far as they have a bearing on the story line itself, the two important factors in these chapters are Philip's steadily worsening financial position and his acquaintanceship with Thorpe Athelny.

Maugham has steadily emphasized that Philip is spending more than he can afford; his generosity to Mildred, and unexpected expenses such as the funeral of Cronshaw, are eating into his capital. He will earn no money until he has completed his education, and this is still some years away. This fact should be kept in mind, for it will loom as a major factor shortly.

The second and more pleasant one is Thorpe Athelny, who will play an important role in the story from here on.

NOTES

White Man's Burden
Maugham has somewhat sarcastically put this in capitals. In these days Britain still had colonies, and when a man from a family with some means got into trouble, he was shipped overseas to carry the "burden" among the natives."

Smoking Concerts
Smokers, all-male parties.

Shake Down
British slang expression meaning a place to sleep.

Gallipot
A small bottle used for holding drugs.

Hospital
Dr. Tyrell says: "A hospital is a charitable institution." This was exactly what it was at the time. No one who could afford medical care was examined or admitted.

Got It
The reference is to tuberculosis.

St. Moritz
Again the reference is to tuberculosis sanitariums in the Swiss Alps.

Rolling
Rolling in money. The slang is the same as the American.

Advance of Royalties
A sum of money that a publisher reluctantly gives an author on acceptance of his work. It is applied against whatever monies the book may earn, and is immediately deducted thereon.

62

Barrel Organ
A sort of portable player-piano that was held by a cord around the neck and cranked by hand.

Proofs
Printers' proofs, the galleys which the author and proofreader will check for changes and corrections before final printing.

Dresser
A surgeon's assistant in a hospital.

Two Diseases
The reference is to venereal diseases.

Gas About You
Talk too much.

Talipes
The Latin for club-foot.

Sovereign
A gold one pound coin, called this because the face on it was of the monarch of the time.

Press Representative
An advertising copy writer

Black Letter
Gothic or Old English type, of the kind seen on wedding announcements.

Board-School
A school under the management of the school board, what we call a public school in this country.

CHAPTERS LXXXVII THROUGH LXXXIX

SUMMARY

After Athelny leaves the hospital Philip goes to dine with him on a Sunday. The Athelnys live in an old and shabby house but the family, consisting of Athelny and his wife and nine children, is a happy one and Philip spends a pleasant day. Athelny has done many things in his lifetime, and is quite frank about his failure to make good in any of them. He is a voluble and interesting talker and he excites Philip's interest by telling him of his long stay in Spain. Philip is invited to come again the next Sunday for dinner, but because he fears the Athelnys cannot really afford to have him, he drops in later for tea, bringing a large cake. The children take to Philip, and except for the oldest, Sally, who is a reserved 15, all call him Uncle Philip after a time. Soon Philip develops the habit of going to the Athelnys every Sunday.

COMMENT

In this interlude that might be called a bridge between one major part of the plot and another, Philip makes the acquaintance of the Athelny family. It is not without significance, as will become evident later.

The Athelnys are important insofar as they show Philip that a family can be happy as a unit without having much money. As Philip himself observes, this is the first time in his lonely life that he has been present in a family circle. The Athelny children take to Philip, for they can feel that he is truly fond of them. He is flattered and touched by their affection.

This is a charming, diversionary part of the novel, but it should be remembered that Maugham, while often called a cynic who sees only the base part of human nature, is nothing of the sort. He cannot stand the false, the phony, and this he will attack unmercifully, but toward those people who are sincere, whether they be saint or sinner, he shows the deepest respect. We never do find out whether the bombastic little Athelny is really all that he says he was, but the point Maugham makes is what does it really matter. Athelny is a good and kind man and if he wishes to paint himself in false colors in order to impress others, he is hurting no one. While Athelny is not Cronshaw, there is a similarity in that they are both failures, but honest failures. Maugham is kind to them.

The playwright continues to set his scenes. Without divulging what will come later, this Athelny episode is by no means simply a side road of the main plot. It is also another of the happy heights that contrast with the sad lows in Philip's life. The roller-coaster is still running.

NOTES

"Punch"
A famous British humor magazine that has been published for a very long time and is still going strong.

Bad Drains
Plumbing, something for which Britain is not noted even today.

Yorkshire Pudding
The Oxford English Dictionary defines this as: "A batter-pudding cooked under a joint of meat or in meat juice," which makes little sense to

an American. It is a non-sweet sort of pancake that is almost inevitably eaten with roast beef in Britain.

Jug of Beer

It was common practice to go to the neighborhood "pub" or tavern and buy a pitcher or jug of draft beer. In the United States in days past the container was called a "growler," and from it came the expression "growler rushing," meaning to drink.

Pudding

This is not Yorkshire Pudding, but a sweet concoction made of rice and sugar and raisins.

Ices

The forerunner of ice cream. Sherbets and the like.

Uppers

In poor financial straits.

El Greco

Domenico Teotocopulo, the Greek-born painter who settled in Spain in the 16th century. He painted strange and disturbing pictures that were different from anything that had been attempted before. Today, some critics believe he may have been extremely short-sighted, the reason for some of his distortions. In any case, he was the most revolutionary of the so-called masters, and his influence on later generations of artists has been considerable.

Cottage Loaf

A small loaf.

Walking Out

Couples walking together, a date.

Puts Her Hair Up

The age varied, but when a girl no longer wore her hair in braids, or simply hanging down, it was a sign that she was a grown woman.

Sub-Editor

A British sub-editor is what is called a copy reader in the United States. His job is to edit the copy that reporters turn in and to write headlines.

CHAPTERS XC THROUGH XCVII

SUMMARY

One evening as Philip is returning from dinner at the Athelnys he runs into Mildred again. He discovers that she is now a streetwalker, and while he is disgusted and shocked, he feels a great pity for her. He suggests that if she will give up the life she can come and live in his apartment and take over the simple duties he has been hiring a woman to do. Mildred and her little girl move in to Philip's spare room, and Philip is happy that he is able to do something for Mildred, but his old passion is gone. Mildred is unable to understand this; now she is not only willing but anxious to give herself to him, for the physical is the only relationship with a man that Mildred understands. Philip is fond of the baby, and for her sake, and for the love he once had for Mildred, is willing to support them, but that is all. One night Mildred tries her utmost to get Philip to sleep with her, but he is disgusted and shakes her off. This makes Mildred furious. She calls Philip every vile name she can think of and ends with the epithet she knows will hurt him the most: "cripple!" Mildred is not around when Philip gets up the next day to go to the hospital. When he returns he finds that his apartment is in shambles, the furniture slashed, dishes broken, bedclothes ripped. Mildred and the baby are gone. Philip is amazed at the damage, and while he feels a sense of material loss, is glad to be finally rid of Mildred. He is sad that he will no longer see the baby, but realizes that the child will soon forget him. He salvages what he can from the wreckage and moves into a cheap room, convenient to the hospital. This is important, for his funds are running dangerously low.

COMMENT

This is the next to last act in the story of Philip and Mildred. Philip is emotionally rid of her now, but being a decent person, he cannot be insensible to Mildred's plight. Also, as Maugham hints, people do acts of kindness not so much for others, but for their own satisfaction. When Philip takes in Mildred, now a streetwalker, he cannot help feeling noble, and this is a dangerous emotion.

Mildred is now the one who is grateful, at least for the time being. Note that this word has been used before: Philip was grateful to Norah, but he was not in love with her.

Mildred is quite naturally puzzled at Philip's new attitude toward her. Formerly she had had no difficulty in handling Philip under any circumstances, and now that she is willing to give him what he so desperately wanted before, she cannot understand why he will not take her. As Maugham has shown us, she is a common, stupid woman, and she only knows men as creatures of passion. A Philip that no longer desires her is something new, and it bothers her terribly.

Philip, we gather, is not repelled by Mildred because she has become a streetwalker. He is not censuring her for becoming one, realizing that in order to support her baby she had very little choice. But Philip's love is now dead, and he can look only on the obsession he suffered from as a sort of disease from which he has now been cured. The intensity of the passion he once had is now the intensity of his loathing.

The Brighton interlude is interesting in showing the contrast between the last time that Philip and Mildred had been there. Philip once danced attendance on Mildred after he sent her to Brighton following the birth of the baby; he was eager for her to recover from her confinement so that he could take her off to Paris on a "honeymoon." It is now Mildred who is insulted because he refuses to share a room with her. In her twisted manner she calls it "unnatural" and "humiliating." This from Mildred who has been a streetwalker! Philip's reaction is not anger or even annoyance, but simply boredom, and this is the greatest insult of all to Mildred.

After they return to London we have the climactic scene when Mildred tries to seduce Philip. When Mildred breaks down and begs Philip to love her, the scene is one of horror, a reflection of Philip's reaction. Just as Maugham has not spared Philip in the past, he now shows Mildred even more clearly for what she is. It is obvious that while Mildred does not really love Philip (she is probably incapable of such an emotion) she thinks she does. The idea that Philip no longer desires her physically, when in the past he would have done anything to possess her, is incredible to Mildred. She is willing now to debase herself to get what she could have had before with a snap of her fingers.

When she is spurned, the fury that even hell does not have, as Shakespeare tells us, is turned loose on Philip. He listens in astonishment at the vileness of her invective, but he no longer really cares. After the years of emotional torture when he would have been deeply hurt, he is drained of any emotion toward her. He no longer cares.

Mildred's act of vandalism adds nothing to the story, but only emphasizes the low character of Mildred. She can no longer hurt Philip emotionally, and she knows it. As a woman she cannot hurt him physically, and she is probably too much of a coward to resort to murder. So she tries to destroy the few material things that Philip likes. It has been brought out that she objects to Philip displaying some of his nude drawings from his Paris days on the grounds that they are "improper." But her final act of destruction is more than destruction of hated objects; its purpose is to hurt Philip.

Even after viewing the wreckage of his few possessions, we are again told that Philip "did not think of her with wrath, but with an overwhelming sense of boredom." This is the end of whatever remained of Philip's emotional bondage to Mildred.

It is the rare reader who will not sigh with relief at this point. The torment of Philip's spirit is lifted, but the road ahead is still not without its travail.

NOTES

Train
  A long, trailing skirt.

Ladies
The allusion is to "ladies of the night," prostitutes.

Diggings
  Rooms, lodgings.

Service
  Domestic service, to become a maid.

Mellin's Food
  A patented baby formula powder.

Done Up
  Tired.

Kaffir Market
  Kaffir is a reference to South Africa, where the natives were known as
kaffirs. South African stocks, gold mines.

Tram
  British for streetcar.

Go-Cart
  Not the tiny automobile racers of today, but simply a baby carriage.

Rum Customer
  Strange character.

This Little Pig, Etc.
  A British nursery rhyme.

Flutter
  A gamble on the stock market.

Traps
  Luggage.

Along the Front
  The boardwalk by the sea.

Hopping
Picking hops, an ingredient that goes into beer.

Mid-Wifery
Obstetrics, bringing babies into the world.

Tramp
A steamer with no scheduled stops that picks up cargo and takes it to any destination.

Well of the Theater
The center of the lecture hall where the operation is performed, while the students sit above it on tiers watching.

War
The war referred to here is the Boer or South African war between the British and the Dutch settlers in what is now the Union of South Africa. It lasted from 1899 to 1902, and turned out to be a bit more than the British had bargained on. The Boers, or Africans, were extremely tough fighters, and gave the British no end of trouble. Winston Churchill was a war correspondent in South Africa, and at one time the Boers had a price on his head for his death or capture.

Iodoform
An iodine (antiseptic) powder that was much used before the days of sulfa and antibiotics.

Wicket
A small gate or door.

Mug
A stupid fool.

Going Out
Going to the war, going overseas.

Basin and Ewer
At this period, before the days of running water in most houses, it was common to have a large porcelain basin and an ewer—a pitcher—in the bedroom in order to wash one's face and hands.

CHAPTERS XCVIII THROUGH CII

SUMMARY

Philip now reaches the lowest point in his fortunes. The Macalister's suggested stock deal backfires, and Philip finds that, after paying off on the stock he had bought on margin, he is left with only seven pounds. He writes to his uncle for help but is turned down. He is desperate and does not know what to do. Unable even to pay his modest rent, he takes to wandering the streets and he knows hunger for the first time in his life. He looks for employment, but he has no experience, and there are many others looking for work. Finally, he goes to the Athelnys for Sunday dinner, after having missed a week in the regular routine. Philip pretends that nothing is amiss, but Athelny, who has long known poverty, is not fooled. He pries the story out of Philip, then insists that he live with the family until he gets back on his feet. Philip is deeply touched. In a short time, thanks to Athelny, he manages to get a job in the shop where Athelny works as a copywriter.

COMMENT

These chapters depict a period in Philip's life when he hits rock bottom financially. Maugham shows us poverty as it concerns Philip, a young man who has always had something even if it wasn't a great deal. Now Philip discovers what it is to be completely penniless. Because he has had no experience with such a state of affairs, he is helpless. Philip looks for a job, but we feel that he does not really want one. He is vaguely hoping for some miracle to happen and cannot believe that the condition he finds himself in is real.

This rather strange state of affairs is understandable if one considers the circumstances in which Philip has grown up. Maugham shows us that the English gentleman of the time, if deprived of his income, however modest it might have been, was a helpless character. Nothing in his past life has prepared him for such an eventuality. This is a state of mind the young people of Britain and the United States probably will find hard to understand today. But it was a condition that many an American found himself in during the Great Depression. That was not too many years ago, and John Steinbeck's *Grapes of Wrath,* for instance, may sound dated, but it was much too realistic for comfort to those who read it when it was first published.

Philip first turns to his uncle for help. He is turned down and this certainly does nothing to change Philip's feelings towards him. But the Vicar stays in character. He still hands out homilies and platitudes but not kindness or money.

Maugham shows us that Philip discovers a very unpleasant truth, that when the chips are down, there are very few people who will help you. Maugham must have found out early in his career that it is easy to sneer at money but it is difficult to get along without it. Maugham makes no bones of the fact that he wrote for money. Once he had made it as a playwright he was able to indulge in the luxury of writing what he wished. This is that book.

Maugham does not pity Philip; he shows him in the same pitiless light as he did in the Mildred sequences. Philip is still immature and has much to learn. He has gone through the emotional mill; now he must go through the financial. But at the same time Philip is developing one characteristic that Maugham dwells on: Philip is able to appraise himself as well as those around him. (This is, of course, Maugham himself. It is evident in all his writing, and in this semi-autobiography he stresses it.)

Philip is able to look at Lawson and to realize that the portrait painter is nothing more than an acquaintance he has known for some time. He realizes that he would probably get a handout from Lawson, but that any real help would not be forthcoming. His analysis is probably quite correct.

But now succor comes from an unexpected quarter. Maugham is not saying that poverty breeds nobility of character—far from it. He simply shows that there are people in this world who have a deep sense of kindness and will display it to the limit of their resources when the occasion arises.

Athelny comes through as a truly kind man. Maugham has shown us a rather ridiculous little man, strutting in his "robes of assumption," but the clown turns out to be the true friend. Where the others have failed him completely, Athelny comes through. The aid is voluntarily offered, which makes it doubly welcome.

Chapter CI is rather a sentimental passage for Maugham, but it again demonstrates that he is not the cynic that he is often accused of being. (The appellation, one gathers from reading other works of Maugham, is not distasteful to Maugham. He would probably refer the name-caller to the first definition in the dictionary under "cynic.") Maugham admires honesty and integrity, and here in a subtle way he gives fulsome praise to a real and generous man and his wife.

Note that Maugham has since Chapter LXXXVI, when Philip first meets Athelny, been paving the way for Athelny's act of compassion. It should not come as a surprise to the reader. At the same time Maugham is taking a slap at middle class morality and middle class genteelism. Athelny is actually an aristocrat, as Maugham sees him. He may be a bogus one so far as birth is concerned, and Maugham has hinted at this, but an aristocrat, in Maugham's lexicon has nothing to do with birth. It is a person who has what genteel people would call intestinal fortitude. This is what H. W. Fowler would call a "genteelism." Maugham would prefer the honest if vulgar term "guts."

NOTES

Lost on the Playing Fields

Maugham twists the Duke of Wellington's famous statement about how the Battle of Waterloo (1814) was won on the playing fields of Eton, a reference to the gallant British officers who came from the public school caste. In South Africa, the descendants of these gallant officers were just as gallant, but they were up against an enemy who believed it was better to win than be gallant. When the Boer War started, the British still wore scarlet coats that stood out wonderfully — the Boer sniper's viewpoint — against the African terrain. The Boers wore khaki, which wasn't so glamorous but far more efficient.

Colossus

The reference is to Great Britain, on whose colonies the sun never set at the time. (British soldiers also switched to khaki.)

Account

The reference here is to what we call margin stock transaction. The Securities Exchange Commission is quite strict nowadays, but at this period in Britain stock could apparently be bought on margin for nothing down if you knew the broker. The catch was that if it went down, you were required to cover. In other words, if you bought 100 shares at $10 apiece and they then went down a point, you were required to put up $100; if on the other hand it went up a point and you sold, you would receive $100, minus the broker's commission.

Differences

Macalister's reference to differences is what has been explained above.

Cape

The Cape of Good Hope, South Africa. Capetown is the city.

Yeomanry

County militia, mobilized in time of war. Philip's boss when he was apprenticed as an accountant, Mr. Carter, was an officer in a yeomanry regiment. A trooper is a cavalryman.

Gene

French for circumstances, in this reference an unpleasant experience.

Cropper

A heavy fall, generally financial.

Reversion

In this case it refers to the possibility of borrowing money against a will that is used as collateral.

Victoria, Charing Cross, etc.

Railway stations in London. Public washrooms were available and this is where Philip goes to clean up.

Buyer

In this context, a departmental manager. Buyers also buy on the wholesale market, and this is where they get their name.

Roll-Desk

A roll-top desk, rarely seen nowadays.

Governor

The boss.

Cue

A waiting line, generally spelled queue in this country.

Veldt

The plains of South Africa.

Big Ben

The famous clock on the tower of the Parliament buildings in London. It appears briefly at the beginning of every Arthur Rank Production British motion picture.

Son of Levi

A not too flattering reference to a Jew.

Wrote to You, etc.

Postal service was and is excellent in Britain. It may be of interest to note that a letter mailed in the morning before 10 o'clock in London will be delivered in another part of the city before four in the afternoon.

Found

Board and lodging.

CHAPTERS CIII THROUGH CIX

SUMMARY

Philip enters into the life of a shopwalker in a linendrapers, a shop that sells cloth and women's clothes. He lives in a dormitory with the other clerks, and he eats with them. It is a miserable existence compared to what he has known in the past, but at least he has a place to eat and sleep and earns a few shillings a week. In time, his drawing ability stands him in good stead and he is "promoted" to designer, although he receives no raise in pay. Once a week he drops in at the hospital to see if there is any mail for him from his uncle or his old associates, and one day he finds a letter from Mildred saying she is in trouble and asking him to come and see her. At first he has no intention of doing so, but next day he changes his mind and looks her up. She is staying in a shabby lodging house in a sordid district. Mildred tells him that there is something wrong with her, but she does not want to go to the hospital for an examination. Philip examines her; he finds that she has syphilis, and he prescribes some medicine for her. He tells her she must give up what she is doing, but discovers shortly that she is continuing as a streetwalker. Philip pleads in vain, and finally he says to himself: "I can't do anything more." He never sees Mildred again.

COMMENT

Emotionally, Philip is now free, but he has been reduced to the status of a shopwalker and he sees nothing ahead for himself unless his uncle dies and leaves him enough money to continue his medical education. Maugham shows us the miserable existence of an ordinary white collar worker in London at the time. The contrast with conditions today will make the reader realize how far we have advanced in employee-employer relations since the turn of the century. Contrasted to the last time that Philip worked as an apprentice in an accountant's firm, he is now nothing but an ordinary clerk.

Philip is anxious for his uncle to die. There is no sentiment in his emotions; he is quite bluntly ghoulish. Philip has never cared for his uncle, and when the Vicar refuses to help him, his feelings become more intense. Philip's desire is a perfectly normal one as Maugham depicts it.

Although it has no particular bearing on the story, Philip meets Lawson for what is to be the last time and hears from him that Hayward had died shortly after reaching South Africa. This is Maugham's last little bit of irony insofar as the shiftless Hayward is concerned; his enlistment as a soldier was possibly the only thing he had done in his life which had any significance. If he had been killed in battle, the end of his life might have had some meaning, but instead he dies of some intestinal disease. Even his death is wasted. Maugham continues to close the doors on Philip's past life. Presently they will be completely shut.

When Philip receives the letter from Mildred, the ambivalent feeling he has for her is again evident. At first he cares not at all about Mildred's troubles, but he then begins to worry. He can never rid himself of her completely; he has been scarred too deeply.

Maugham has dragged Philip down to the status of a clerk in a "shop." The once financially independent Philip who could give Mildred little luxuries is now able to give her only a prescription and advice she will not take. But even this is something, and as usual, it is Philip who is doing the giving.

While Maugham does not come out and say so, the symptoms which Mildred displays are clear evidence of syphilis. It should be borne in mind that this book was first published in 1915, and while it was quite a shocker in its time, venereal diseases were still not mentioned by name in print. In fact, right up to the time quite recently that a national magazine in the United States campaigned for frankness, they were referred to as "social" diseases.

This was before the days of the wonder drugs, and while with proper treatment over a long period of time, syphilis could be arrested if not cured completely, it amounted to a death sentence if not treated. Philip impresses this on Mildred, but she is too far gone in her life as a prostitute to care any more.

In a passing reference we learn that Mildred's baby has died. Mildred, who knows that Philip was very fond of the little girl, is shocked when he says that he is glad to hear it. This again is the difference between Philip, by now a realist and, we gather, a quite decent character, and Mildred, a mess of "genteel" (using the blacker connotation of the word), insincere feelings, able to rationalize anything, even including her whoredom.

In another indirect reference to Philip's character, when Mildred, to whom such a feeling would be natural, tells Philip that now he has had his revenge, he gets no satisfaction whatsoever. Revenge is a cheap emotion, Maugham indicates, and Philip is above it. What is more, Philip has gone through enough sorrow himself, and is reaching his majority.

Mildred is a rather pitiful character now, and Maugham treats her compassionately. Perhaps it was inevitable from the start that she would end up a diseased prostitute. She is in the gutter, and Maugham treats the beaten kindly. The final parting is, in many ways, a rather poignant one. Mildred, once so arrogant, is reduced to nothing. Philip, while he has his own troubles, is now a man. The contrast is tragic.

And now the door is closed.
"That was the end. He did not see her again."
Philip's bondage is over at long last.

NOTES

Frock Coat
A double-breasted coat with long skirts which are the same in length in front as behind.

Salt Cellars
Containers for salt, not shakers.

'Store'
A reference to a private stock of condiments, jams and so forth.

Bath Bun
A large fruit bun with a sugared top. Possibly named after the town of Bath, a famous health resort.

Stopped for Washing
Withheld for laundry charges.

Sweater
A tailor, not the garment.

Sidey
British slang for conceited.

Sen-Sens
Perfumed little tablets, violet-colored, that are supposed to sweeten the breath.

Whist
The antecedent of the card game of bridge. Bridge, particularly contract bridge, is a fairly recent invention.

Beano
A party, a social gathering.

Degage
Detached, unconstrained manner.

Five Bob
Bob is a common term for a shilling. Hence, five shillings.

Remainder
Books left over after an edition has been printed. They are sold at a discount to get them out of the way.

Serio-Comic
Literally, partly serious and partly comic. Performers like Red Skelton can be called serio-comics.

Give Her the Sick
Made her sick, disgusted her.

Decolletage
Exposure, showing of bosom.

CHAPTERS CX AND CXI

SUMMARY

Philip goes to see his uncle during the Christmas holidays. The old man is very ill but hangs grimly on to life. Philip is anxious for him to die, for this will make it possible for him to resume his medical education and escape from the hated shop. He even thinks of giving the Vicar an overdose of drugs, but cannot bring himself to do so. He returns to London and the shop, and it is not until July that he is summoned to Blackstable. This time his uncle is definitely dying, and Philip watches the last moments of a man's life fading away. He is amazed at the tenacity to cling to life and he is also surprised to find how religion can comfort a man at the end.

COMMENT

When Maugham at the end of Chapter CIX says, "That was the end," it is virtually the end of the story. Everything that comes afterwards is anticlimatic.If this were not a semi-autobiographical work, Maugham the craftsman would probably have ended it right there. But he apparently felt that he should continue the story of Philip to such a place as he could pick up the odds and ends and give the reader some idea of what will come in Philip's life. It adds little to the main story of one man's bondage.

In these two chapters, Philip watches his uncle die. It is not a pretty tale, and Maugham bares the soul of man. While Philip literally contemplates murder, the essential decency of his character makes it impossible for him to do so. But Maugham does show us how desperate a person can become when frustrated.

When Philip returns for the death watch, he is only interested in how long it will be before he will come into his inheritance so he can resume again his life as a medical student. He does not care one whit about his uncle, but as he watches him die, a change comes over Philip. He is filled with pity at how meaningless a man's life can be. Maugham echoes John Donne's famous lines: "...any man's death diminishes me, because I am involved in mankind; and therefore never seem to know for whom the bell tolls; it tolls for thee." Maugham does not actually quote from Donne, but Philip's sentiments reflect this point of view. "What a price it was to pay for being other than the beasts!" Again, Maugham sees some good in man even when he is at his lowest.

An understanding of this great Maugham novel makes it much easier to grasp the philosophy he broadcasts in all his other works. Man, says Maugham, is essentially greedy, scheming, evil, vile, and cruel. But not-withstanding, there can be a nobility in him. Man is used here in the generic sense, and although individuals can be thoroughly rotten, this is not true of man in general. In all of Maugham's writings there is a sense of compassion. He will rip and tear a character apart, but he will treat with kindness those whose failings are only of the flesh. The Vicar, a "stupid, hard man, eaten up with a small sensuality," is laid gently to rest by Maugham.

NOTES

Master Philip
A servant referring to a member of the household would call a young man by his first name, prefixed by "master."

Boxing Day
The day after Christmas. It is called this because it is the day on which Christmas "boxes," or presents, are given.

Outre
Daring, different, or as we might say today, "way out."

In the Street
Fired, out of work.

Communion
The British High Church follows the Roman Catholic ritual and the communion that the Vicar receives is similar to the Catholic last rites. It is given only after confession.

Bluebottle
A large housefly.

CHAPTERS CXII THROUGH CXXII

SUMMARY

After his uncle's funeral, Philip returns to London to continue his medical education. Working as an obstetrical assistant, he sees a great deal of the life of the very poor and discovers that they need not be pitied for they accept their fate. On completion of his studies he receives his diploma and plans to take a holiday in Spain. But in the meantime he accepts a post as an assistant to a crusty old country doctor who takes a liking to him and offers him a partnership. Philip has other plans, however, for he wants to become a ship's doctor and see the world. During a brief holiday he goes to the hop fields in Kent to visit the Athelnys. On a sudden impulse one night he makes love to Sally, the oldest Athelny girl. Sally, in her usual serene way, accepts him completely. She indicates that she has been in love with Philip for some years. Later, in London, she tells Philip she may be pregnant and Philip sees all his hopes of traveling going out the window. He decides to make the sacrifice and marry Sally, although he does not love her. In answer to his own wire, he receives a telegram from the old doctor telling him the partnership is still open. But he meets Sally again and she tells him that everything is all right. Philip feels he is again free, but suddenly there is no satisfaction in the freedom. He realizes that what he really wants is love and a family life. Philip proposes to Sally, and she accepts as the book ends.

COMMENT

These concluding chapters contain a good deal of Maugham's philosophy of life. Maugham, in the person of Philip, has been learning constantly. The trials and tribulations Philip has endured have now finally brought him to manhood, and he is able to look about him and view things objectively.

Maugham depicts for us the sordid, hopeless life of the very poor in London at this period. (It may indicate one reason why Britain is today a welfare state.) Maugham's conclusion is that the very poor accept their lot in life, and he takes a few slaps at social workers and others who try to change their way of living. The analysis may or may not be correct, but it is a penetrating and interesting one.

The story itself — the main plot — is now coasting downhill. As pointed out before, everything that happens after Chapter CIX is strictly anticlimatic.

Maugham's tone in these chapters is one of happiness, as though he had purged himself by writing of Philip's miseries. This is undoubtedly the case, and if this were a musical composition, might be compared to the last movement of Beethoven's Ninth Symphony where the chorus sings triumphantly of Elysium.

There are two factors that account for Philip's happiness. Philip is emotionally free of his obsession for Mildred, and while Maugham mentions that Philip will never be completely rid of her in his mind, he sees the relationship with her now only as a horrible period in his life that is forever behind him. Financially, the Vicar's death again puts Philip in a position where he can have small comforts. It is possible for him now to finish his medical education, and we gather that he will have a small sum left over for emergencies. Armed with a medical degree and a few pounds in reserve, the future is bright.

Philip now has only one tie with the past, and this is a fairly recent past. The Athelnys are his only friends. Hayward is dead, and Philip has no desire to see Lawson again.

Maugham has built up a picture of a poor but happy household at the Athelnys. The character of Sally, the oldest, was brought out as we went along, and she is now a grown woman. Note how Maugham was carefully laying the scene. Maugham draws a rather idealistic picture of her, and while she emerges as a thoroughly admirable and pleasant person, the image is somewhat blurred. Sally, one suspects, is not a real character, but one that Maugham cut out of whole cloth. Maugham is never at his best when he invents a character; he is too much the reporter to be able to completely fictionalize. The reader will have a difficult time forgetting Mildred. Every facet of her character should be etched in his mind. Mildred is real, but Sally is something out of a fairy tale. She is wonderful, but one somehow wonders if such a woman can exist.

Here at last, however, Maugham strikes a balance. For the first time Philip is loved and at the end returns the love. This, Maugham seems to stress, is the way it must be. All other emotional episodes in Philip's life have been one-sided.

Maugham is singing his paean and can be forgiven for becoming a bit "corny" at this stage. We gather that Philip and Sally will marry and go to live in the country "happily ever after." It is a pleasant ending to the story of one man's travail.

NOTES

Precincts
The area around a cathedral, the fields.

Bat at the Nets
A bat is used in cricket, like in baseball, although it is quite different in shape. The nets apparently refer to a practice area, like a batting cage in baseball.

Dripping
The reference here is to bread that has been dipped in the juice from roast beef or possibly fried in bacon fat.

District Visitor
Social worker.

Builder
A construction foreman.

80

Regular Caution
British slang for quite a character.

Stout
Strong beer-like beverage.

See Her Through
See her through the birth of the baby.

"Decline and Fall"
Edward Gibbon's famous "Decline and Fall of the Roman Empire."

Banns be Called
Public notice given in church of an intended marriage. Common practice in the Church of England; if any of the parishioners had an objection, they spoke up.

Locum
In this case, a substitute doctor.

Crab in It
What's the catch?

Asepsis
Precautions for the exclusion of bacteria. Differing from antisepsis, where antiseptics are used after the operation. It should be remembered that Dr. South had received his education at a time when Pasteur and Lister were still to be heard from.

Fagged
Tired.

Sprats
A small fish. Can be of several species.

Port
A sweet wine from Portugal, specifically from Oporto, hence the name. It was the custom among British gentlemen then, and still is, to drink a glass or two or three or four—or even a few bottles, from which habit comes the term "Three Bottle Man"—after dinner.

Swede From a Mangel Wurzel
A swede is a type of turnip and a mangel wurzel a beet.

Lucullus
A wealthy Roman famous for the luxury of his banquets, hence Lucullan, luxurious in relation to food.

Brillat-Savarin
A famous French chef, author of a cookbook.

Kippers
Kippered herring, salted and smoked fish often eaten in Britain for breakfast.

Oast-Hous
A building containing a kiln for drying hops.

Licencee
The owner of a tavern. Note the British "c" spelling.

York and Lancaster
The rival houses of York and Lancaster that fought the Wars of the Roses for the throne of England from 1455 to 1485. Lancaster, in the person of Edward VII, finally came out on top, but as he married Elizabeth of York, the houses became united. The white and red rose was respectively the symbol of the houses of York and Lancaster.

Sweet William
A flower, a species of pink, related to the carnation.

Love-in-a-Mist
An aromatic grass, also the Fennel flower.

London Pride
Also the Sweet William. Maugham repeats himself.

Trade Entrance
The entrance through which the employees entered and left.

P. & O.
The Peninsular and Oriental Line, a famous British shipping company still very much in existence.

Tokio
This is Tokyo, the capital of Japan. The British used to spell it this way, and probably still do. They still refer to Thailand as Siam and Iran as Persia!

Pleased as Punch
Why someone should be as pleased as Punch, who was always being hit over the head by Judy, is a puzzle, but the British saying means "to be very pleased."

QUESTIONS AND SUGGESTIONS FOR THEMES:

1. What is the impression you receive from Maugham's description of British public school life? How does Philip react to it? Write a theme comparing British public school life of this period with that in an American public school today, taking into account the scholastic, disciplinary, teacher-student relationship, and other factors.

2. What, if anything, does Philip learn in Heidelberg? Does his stay in Germany help in his character development? Write a theme comparing life in the pension in Heidelberg and the vicarage in Blackstable.

3. What is Philip's emotional reaction to his affair with Miss Wilkinson? How would you classify Miss Wilkinson: comic, tragic, pitiful, gay, loose? Write a theme on what you think this love affair means to Philip and Miss Wilkinson.

4. What is the difference between an articled clerk and an ordinary clerk in an accountant's office? Write a theme giving your ideas of the impression you get of the British social structure of this period from Maugham's description of the accountant's office and what has transpired earlier in the story.

5. Of the three art students, Fanny Price, Clutton, and Lawson, which is the talented one, the competent one, and the incompetent one? Is any one of the three a combination of the above descriptions? Write a theme on what you think Maugham means by these three terms.

6. What is Cronshaw's profession? What does Philip think of Cronshaw's poetry? Write a theme on the so-called Bohemian life in Paris as Maugham describes it.

7. How does Philip like his stay in Paris? How does he react to being told he has no future as an artist? Why is he shocked at Fanny Price's suicide? Write a theme on what you think Maugham's views are toward those who try to pursue a career in the arts when they are unsuited for it.

8. What does Philip tell his uncle he learned in Paris? What is his uncle's reaction? Write a theme on what Philip thinks he actually learned in Paris.

9. What makes Philip decide to take up the study of medicine? Was the decision made on his own volition? Write a theme on your impression of the study of medicine in Britain at this time.

10. What is Mildred when Philip first meets her? What is Philip's first impression of Mildred? Write a theme enlarging on this and detailing the contrasts, as you see it, between Philip and Mildred, socially, educationally, and otherwise.

11. When does Philip fall in love with Mildred? Who is Miller? Write a theme explaining why you think Philip fell in love with Mildred.

12. Why does Philip feel he should not marry Mildred? Why does he propose? Why does Mildred turn him down? What is the reason behind Philip's first break with Mildred? Write a theme on what you believe Mildred thinks of Philip, and expand on the *key phrase* that Mildred uses in describing him.

13. How does Norah Nesbit make her living? What is her marital status? Write a theme comparing the characters of Norah and Mildred.

14. What is the new feeling, in addition to love, that Philip feels toward Mildred when she returns after being deserted by Miller? Write a theme on Philip's break with Norah and bring out some of the things which occurred earlier that have a bearing on the breaking-off of love affairs.

15. What does Mildred plan to do with her baby? Is there a similarity between Philip's affair with Norah and Griffiths' affair with Mildred? Write a theme on Philip's action in giving money to Mildred so she may go off with Griffiths, indicating whether or not you think Maugham has built up a convincing situation.

16. What is the joke (regarding Norah) that the gods play on Philip? What is the last pleasure that Cronshaw refuses to give up? Write a theme on what you know of Cronshaw's character and compare it with that of Leonard Upjohn, the critic.

17. In what country did Athelny spend a good many years? How many children does Athelny have, and what is the name of the oldest? Write a theme on your impression of the Athelny family.

18. What profession does Mildred finally take up? Why does Philip ask Mildred to come and live with him? Write a theme on Philip's new feeling for Mildred and compare it with his feelings over the years.

19. What action of Philip's angers Mildred when they go to stay in Brighton? Has the operation cured Philip's club-foot? Write a theme on Brighton as you visualize it.

20. How does Philip lose his money? What was the war that had a bearing on this loss? Write a theme on why Philip has so much difficulty adjusting to his new condition in life.

21. What is Philip's new job? For what purposes are sums deducted from his wages? Write a theme comparing Philip's life as a shopwalker and when he was an articled clerk.

22. Why is Philip anxious for his uncle to die? What change takes place in the Vicar shortly before his death? Write a theme on Philip's views on religion and how they have developed.

23. What is it that Philip discovers about the very poor in London? Write a theme on what kind of a doctor you think Philip will be, and the reasons why.

24. What kind of medical practice does Dr. South have? What is the offer Dr. South makes to Philip? What is the Athelny family doing in Kent? Write a theme on what you think of the last portion of the novel in comparison to what has gone before.

25. Describe Maugham's literary technique in *Of Human Bondage*. (Style, Characterization, Point of View, Plot Manipulation, Handling of Ideas, etc.)

SELECTED BIBLIOGRAPHY

Cordell, Richard Albert. *William Somerset Maugham,* Toronto, New York: T. Nelson and sons, 1937.

_____*Somerset Maugham: A biographical and critical study,* Bloomington, Ind.: Indiana University Press, 1961.

Jonas, Klaus W. *The Maugham Enigma: Anthology,* New York: Citadel Press, 1954.

_____*The World of Somerset Maugham: An Anthology,* New York: British Book Centre, 1959.

McIver, Claude Searcy. *William Somerset Maugham: a study of technique and literary sources,* Philadelphia: University of Pennsylvania Press, 1936.

Pfeiffer, Karl G. *W. Somerset Maugham; a candid Portrait,* New York: Norton, 1959.

Stott, Raymond Toole. *Maughamiana,* London: Heinemann; New York: Doubleday and Co., 1950.

Towne, Charles Hanson, ed. *W. Somerset Maugham, Novelist, Essayist, Dramatist,* New York: George H. Doran, 1925.

Ward, Richard H. *William Somerset Maugham,* London: Geoffrey Press, 1937.

NOTES

22. Why is Philip anxious for Ferdinand's love? What change takes place in the Tsou shortly before his death? Why is he so like on Plato's view of passion and how they have developed?

32. Why is Tintin/Phillip there and why does very keen in London? Write as a team on what to do and do you find... Philip will be sad for however else...

34. What kind of nature of our nation's best doubt how doubtful of the most? Dr. Socu makes put more Wordsworth, Milton, writing... at Keats? Write a drama or drama with impact of the real portion of history an comparison of such the early theme...

25. Describe Margherita Heinz Ferdinand... of Thomas Landauer. 1970's conversations... Congestion in East 1914. Washington, Counting of Terrorism.

SELECTED BIBLIOGRAPHY

Conrad, Richard. Neo-Freudian toward Abounding practic. New York: Dryden and sons, [?].

———. Interpretation of history, in the construction of the Person. London: Janus publics language Press, [?].

Jones, Dr. N... Annabelle's spirit, [?]. London: Oxfords... Ortold Press, [?].

———. The nun in Annabelle's girls, [?]. [?] Washington, New York: Molia town Press, 1939.

Molier, Edoum... Politics of the West. Naturally City to be a naturally academia and in..... Princeton Publications, or republican Press, 1939.

Meana, Patrick G. Language Standards... structure... impact. New York: Prime, 1990.

Shaw, Raymond. Poems of English the London. Home states Free York. Doubleday [?] etc., 1970.

Towards Ports, Edmond. And the Classics.. Maryland... P amid Known in Time. New York: [?] Alfred... 1955.

Ward, Malcolm S. Political thesis of... [?] with London: Confront Press, [?].

NOTES

NOTES

NOTES